The Drawing Center

July 15 – September 2, 2016

Main Gallery

Gabriel de la Mora
Sound Inscriptions on Fabric

Curated by
Brett Littman

DRAWING PAPERS 127

Essays *by* Brett Littman *and* Jace Clayton

Gabriel de la Mora: The Readymade Drawing

Brett Littman

Ever since the first century AD, when Pliny the Elder in his *Natural History* popularized the myth of the sculptor Butades, whose daughter traced her lover's shadow on the wall before he left to war, drawing has been linked to the poetics of the artist's hand and its singular, indexical mark. This origin story of drawing has created a deep interpretative structure wherein the uniqueness of the artist's line and its ability to convey the artist's soul and thoughts has become the dominant way to determine a drawing's importance. Up until the early twentieth century, this system worked pretty well—as drawings were classified as marks on paper made by the artist.

What happens, however, when the artist's hand is removed from the act of drawing? Do you still have a drawing? In 2008, João Ribas curated an exhibition of Rirkrit Tiravanija's *Demonstration Drawings* at The Drawing Center that directly confronted this issue. To create the *Demonstration Drawings*, Tiravanija had commissioned young Thai artists to copy photographs of political protests that had appeared in the *International Herald Tribune* between 2006 and 2007. All of the drawings made by these artists are unsigned, anonymous, and made specifically to exist as part of Tiravanija's open-ended serial drawing archive.

For Ribas, the *Demonstration Drawings* effectively demoted the status of the artist's hand in drawing to a secondary concern. He wrote, "The phenomenology of 'the hand' that so determines the art historical framing of the medium of drawing—in its supposed intimacy or fidelity to thought or intention—is entirely sidelined. Rather, the evocative power of the drawings comes from their ability to turn an ephemeral image of strife or social conflict into a document of political aspiration. Tiravanija's mediation is to take a photojournalistic depiction of an act of political spontaneity and translate it into a medium defined itself by immediacy, both psychological and material."[1]

The *Demonstration Drawings* exhibition was one of the most controversial shows we have ever done. To our general audience it was a heretical act to show drawings attributed to an artist who didn't make them himself. Of course, it seems a bit conservative to me to argue that art not directly made by an artist is not art at all. The twentieth and twenty-first centuries are filled with examples of challenges to authorship, such as readymades, appropriated images, copies, and simulacra. In the case of the *Demonstration Drawings*, I would argue that in many ways it was a perfectly traditional drawing show. The exhibition comprised works on paper made by artists who worked in noticeably different drawing styles and was about mark-making—just not graphics made by Tiravanija.

Gabriel de la Mora's current installation for The Drawing Center, *Sound Inscriptions on Fabric* (2015), moves this problematic one step further. For this series, De la Mora has taken old radio and speaker grills that he purchased at flea markets in Mexico City and presents them as his drawing practice. These are purely readymade drawings that are not manipulated by De la Mora's hand. The form and density of the shaped images that have impregnated the fabric

---

1   João Ribas, "What Would It Mean To Win? Rirkrit Tiravanija's *Demonstration Drawings*," in *Rirkrit Tiravanija: Demonstration Drawings* (New York: The Drawing Center, 2008), 19.

depend on time and the physical structure of each specific speaker. Each of the "inscriptions" document a moment in history, since the patterns were made over years by the sounds of millions of voices, instruments, and even silence passing through the fabric. Can we legitimately call these drawings?

For me (and by extension for The Drawing Center), these are definitely drawings. I have been interested in how drawing can represent the invisible (sound, light, time, energy), and I have been exploring drawing's relationship to sound through graphic scores and also through performance. These works operate as drawings because they visualize time and information through inscription. In addition, *Sound Inscriptions on Fabric* expands De la Mora's interest in recuperating discarded or quotidian objects as the basis for his art. He has gathered extensive collections of materials during his travels around his home town, Mexico City, including shoe soles, aluminum plates for offset printing, doors, erased daguerreotypes, semi-destroyed and compromised paintings, books, badly minted coins, as well as radios, record players, phonographs, and consoles. He classifies all of the artifacts he collects, placing them in his archive so as later to determine which specific items can be designated for projects. I view this archiving function as a metaphor for drawing—one often used by artists to document exploded views and multiple perspectives of one object.

There are many people that I would like to thank for making this exhibition possible. First of all, I would like to acknowledge my colleague Bill Arning, Director of the Contemporary Arts Museum, Houston, who introduced me to Gabriel de la Mora and to this body of work in Mexico City in January 2014. I would also like to recognize the collectors, Jack and Anne Moroniere, who have been championing and collecting Gabriel's work for many years, for their support. I am very grateful for the generosity of Sofía Anaya and Rogelio López; Cecilia Anaya and Enrique Gámez; and Verónica Anaya; as well as José Antonio García Ocejo; Sicardi Gallery, Houston; and the Mexican Agency for International Development Cooperation (AMEXCID) with the Mexican Cultural Institute of New York and the Consulate General Mexico in New York—without their collaboration we could have not have mounted this ambitious installation. Special thanks also to Timothy Taylor, London, and Proyectos Monclova, Mexico City, for all of their help.

I would especially like to thank Jace Clayton for his beautiful and evocative text for this volume. Its mix of the social history of Mexican radio and personal insights makes for a unique and thoughtful rumination on De la Mora's work. From The Drawing Center, I would like to thank Amber Moyles, our Curatorial Assistant; Olga Valle Tetkowski, our Exhibition Manager; Noah Chasin, our Executive Editor; Joanna Ahlberg, our Managing Editor; Peter Ahlberg, AHL&CO; and Alice Stryker, our former Development Director, for all of their help.

Lastly, I would like to thank Gabriel de la Mora and his studio assistants: Marianne Blanco, Jean Espinosa, Alfredo Gallegos, Jorge Hernández, Miguel Hernández, Sandra Martínez, Gladys Mauricio, Karina Mauricio, and Arturo Soto. Their enthusiasm, energy, and highly organized working style has made this a seamless process. Gabriel has been involved in this exhibition every step of the way, and I am very grateful for his intelligence, communication, friendship, and willingness to allow us to show this series at The Drawing Center.

Radio Remains

Jace Clayton

"The Raven *is here to bridge all of us, to mobilize the city's wasted resources. . .*"—EASY THING, PACO IGNACIO TAIBO II

1
RADIO HAPPINESS

I first heard Radio Felicidad (1180AM) crackling out of a decades-old tuner perched on a friend's refrigerator in Mexico City. The suit-jacketed songs of male romance and lament from a departed era formed the perfect soundtrack as my friends and I prepared a huge meal to celebrate Nowrouz, the Iranian New Year. This wasn't an anachronistic pleasure gleaned from listening to old music for ironic effect, nor did it stem from the sentimentalism that we imagined its core audience must have had reminiscing over long-gone days. It would be correct but inaccurate to think of Radio Felicidad's selection of '60s and '70s ballads as being old, or oldies; what they were was *present*. The AM radio broadcast let the city into our late March New

Year's Eve party. The incongruous presence of Radio Felicidad's time-dusted songs rooted us to the place. To enjoy terrestrial radio is to be within reach of some signal tower, to share both time and space with all the other potential listeners. Digital streams and satellite radio offer us a synchronous listening experience, albeit without the sense of spatial intimacy that AM/FM offers.

Between breaks in the music, Radio Felicidad's morning host shares traffic updates, bits of weird and often macabre news from the United States, home remedy information ("try eating a handful of almonds when you feel a migraine coming on"), practical finance advice ("only go to the gas station when your tank is empty, otherwise you'll end up spending extra on snacks and drinks"), and information about workers' organizations. Listening joins me to this wireless public, and that constituency expands my understanding of how one could participate in the city. It's as if the spread of radio reception overlaps with an idea of civic responsibility: we are all in this listening together. Radio does that. It inflects one's experience of a place—soundtrack, tour guide, tipster.

Provided you're in tune with it, radio forms a connective tissue that spreads across a city or region. Borders and crossroads may hold center stage in contemporary discourse but, at least for this listener, the radiant enveloping spaces demarcated by AM/FM radio signals help us to think about reception and responsibility in a different way. Modulation and penumbra articulate presence. There's always a transition zone where static creeps into the signal. You can't just up and leave the broadcast range suddenly. Weather changes receptivity—meaning is environmental, atmospheric. We fiddle with metal and wire amid a field of invisible waves in hopes of boosting input from an adjacent world, and that's precisely what radio is: a body neither celestial nor earthbound but caught up in their intermingling, veined with transmitters and receivers both human and electronic. The visible order of the city ranges from class striations to the brick-and-mortar facts of its topography—at its best, through radio's sensorium we ragtag listeners can experience these hardnesses as pliable and act to shape them. It's an underdog process in an old dog media format. It works the way bass does: when bass frequencies go low enough we lose our ability to perceive what direction the sound is coming from and experience the audio as vibration *in* us: the external slips in. What we hear turns into what we feel. We listen in, sound out, and are moved.

2

SOUND INSCRIPTIONS ON FABRIC

Over the last few years, architect-turned-artist Gabriel de la Mora walked around Mexico City, visiting markets and second-hand stores in search of old radios. Like all places with a violent colonial history, the past here seems excessive, ubiquitous, and endlessly recycled. As the past threatens to overgrow the present, junk markets remind us that those terms themselves are unstable—the past isn't past, but neither is the present particularly present, nor is growth always a change for the better. Market logic and the haggler's jive team up to destabilize any clean division between trash and treasure, and De la Mora works in this zone. When he finds a radio he likes he snaps a photo of it on the spot. Even before buying the radio and transforming it into art, he records its *in situ* image into his personal archive.

These private photographs are forensic in nature; not only do they document the last moments of the radio's lifespan, but they also signal that an autopsy is ready to begin. As the next step, De la Mora dismantles the radio, carefully prizing out the fabric dust-covers sheathing the speakers. Such exhumations of twentieth-century materiality fueled much modernist art, and Minimalism later distilled the process. How stripped down could an artwork become while still being recognizable as such, and do such gestures maintain legibility merely by reinforcing the art world apparatus—gallery, exhibition catalog, critic, and collector?

Here, De la Mora's methodology of selection, documentation, dismantling, and reduction yields fragile rectangles of speaker fabric. These then get trimmed and framed. Each one contains a soiled, ghostly imprint that marks the speaker grill's absence, the soot tracing out operas and ballads and talk shows that were broadcast through the capital's thin, polluted air. The shape and size of the markings allude to the design epoch that produced each radio. They

comprise brown, amber, tan, and blackish dirt accumulations—part
ruin porn, part afterimage, shaped equally by throwaway consumer
histories and by the artist's abstracting hand.

Fifty-five such enclosures comprise De la Mora's solo exhibition at The
Drawing Center, *Sound Inscriptions on Fabric*. They're not portraits
of sounds, nor of sounding-objects. Instead, these dust drawings
constitute a suite of second skins, as if the artist is trying to see what's
underneath the city's traffic and noise and palimpsestic architecture.
All kinds of sociality organize themselves around radio; people install
radios in their cars, in their kitchens, wherever folks gather. Radio
Happiness. How thin a signal do we need to feel connected?

The initial impression of *Sound Inscriptions on Fabric* is one of quiet,
formal minimalism. These works are edged by processes and social
concerns that are not immediately visible but that nevertheless frame
what we see. On one wall, the speaker fabric drawings are arranged
symmetrically, mirrored on either side of a central vertical line. The
arrangement is reminiscent of a family tree, the iconic diagram
format that disallows any messy interpersonal relationships in favor
of the most brute and obvious of connections. On the two flanking
walls the fabric drawings are arranged in a single file, each spaced
fifty centimeters from its neighbor. Regularity pervades; the question
is whether one finds it comforting or clinical.

The process behind *Sound Inscriptions on Fabric* itself forms a stroll
through different types of city-walking: from nineteenth-century
flâneurs to the Situationist *dérive* to the artisanal flea-market bargain
hunters. It ends with the ultimate transformation, that of junk into
art, from near-obsolete (and stubbornly material) media format into
the visual lingua franca of contemporary art in all its fungible glory.
It is also a walk from noise into silence. What began as De la Mora's
stroll through extravagant, aleatory soundfields of Mexico City (where
these radios might still have made noise) ends in the gallery's quiet.

SOLIDARITY RADIO

De la Mora's use of scavenged radios as raw material for art makes me think of Mexico City's most famous fictional late-night radio host, El Cuervo (The Raven) of XEFS's *Las Horas del Cuervo (The Raven's Hours)*. He appears regularly in Paco Ignacio Taibo II's crime novels, and his banter would not sound out of place on Radio Felicidad:

> Here, *Las Horas del Cuervo*, the first and only program of pure solidarity among the nocturna-lazy dogs, vampires, overtime workers, sleepless students, night shift taxi drivers, on-call strikers, prostitutes, luckless thieves, independent detectives, disappointed lovers, die-hard loners, and other creatures of the night.[1]

Taibo II is one of Mexico's most important living writers, and in his series featuring "independent detective" Héctor Belascoarán Shayne, El Cuervo's voice addresses the entire city in his late-night broadcasts. This fantastic audio connectivity is perhaps the novels' most optimistic element—everything else in the books is shot through with a world-weary realism where endurance and a no-nonsense solidarity among the downtrodden are far more important than crime-fighting heroics. Eventually El Cuervo retires to do indigenous language broadcasts in Oaxaca. His mastery of the radio scatters power, as anything that helps the underserved must.

In the first half of the twentieth century, radio's unidirectional information flow was paternalistic at best, totalitarian at worst: state-sponsored messages beamed out from central transmitters to countless receivers. Radio Felicidad and *Las Horas del Cuervo* present an entirely different manifestation of the medium's role. In their world radio remains one of the few things that can unite people across a megalopolis as large and as varied as Mexico City. Gabriel de la Mora's work makes radio's uncanny social fabric visible.

---

[1] This and epigraph from *Cosa Facil*, translation mine.

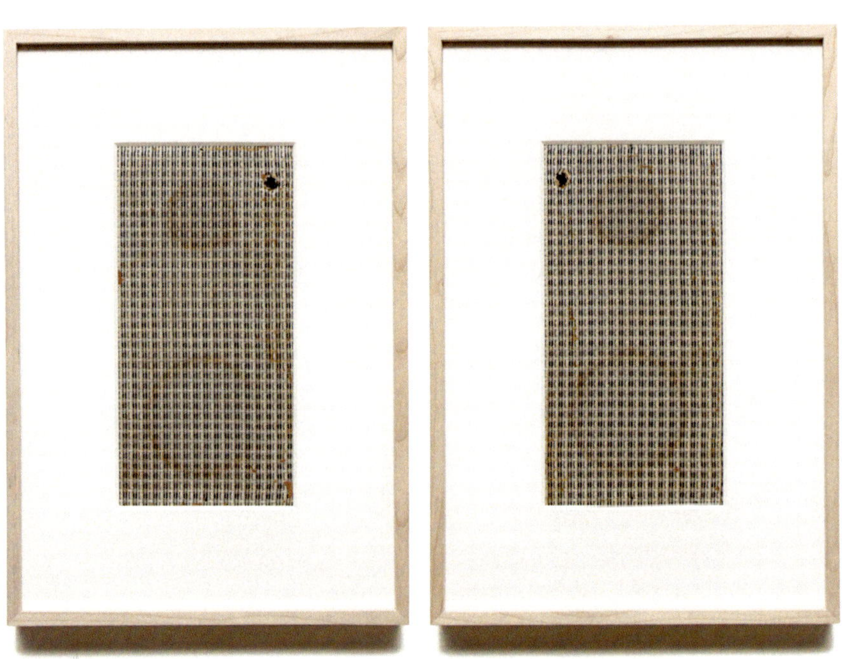

PL. 1
B-17, 2015

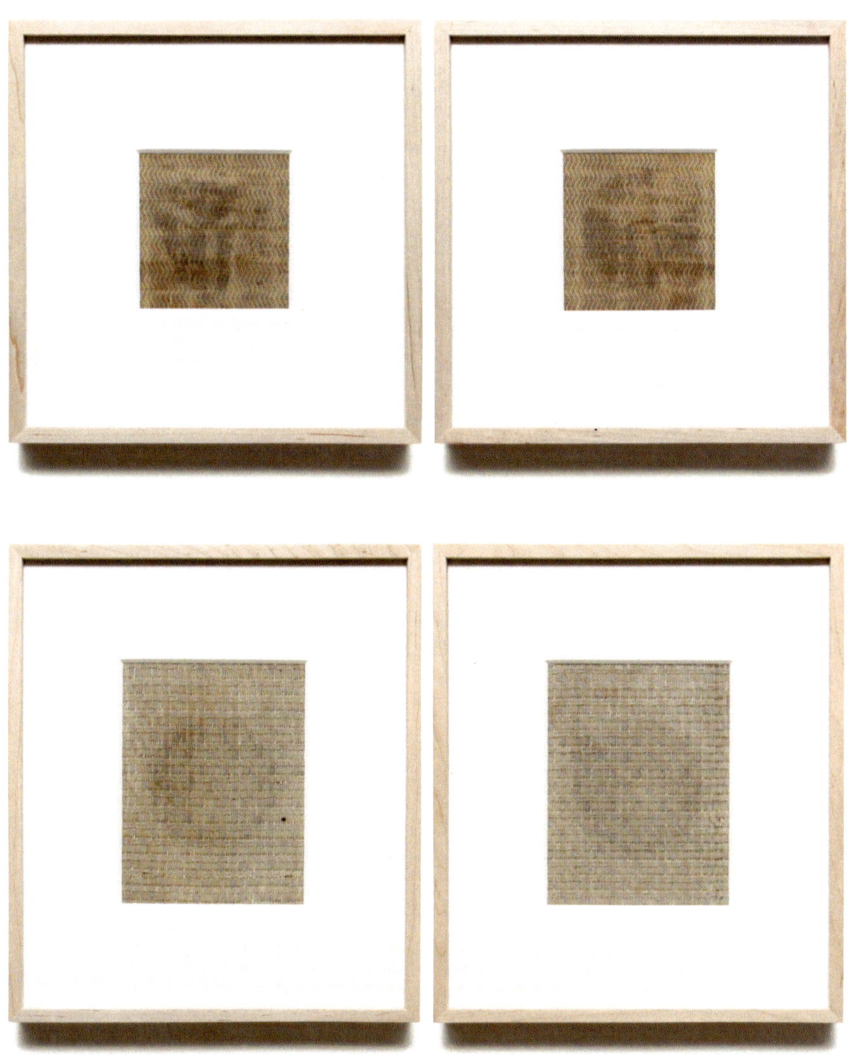

PL. 4
B-37, 2015

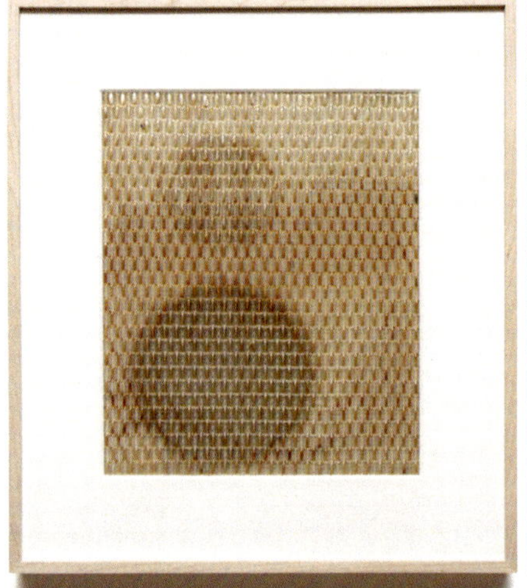 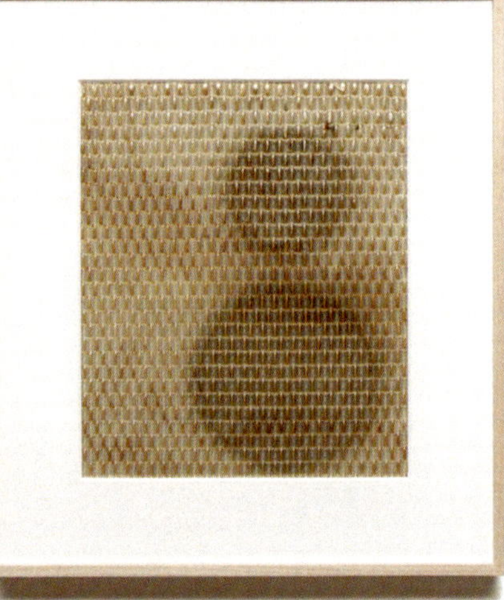

B-39, 2015

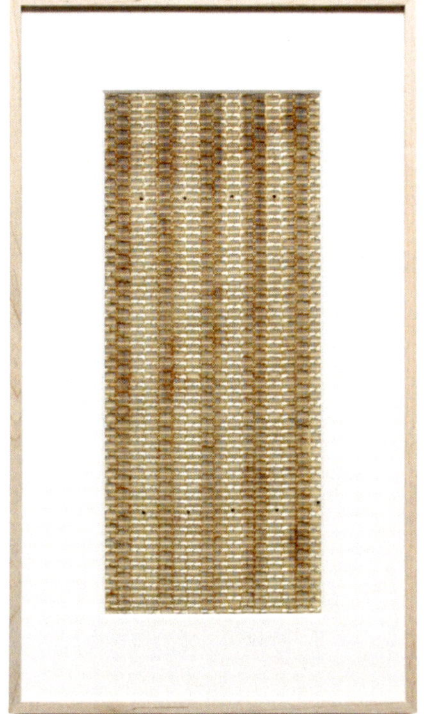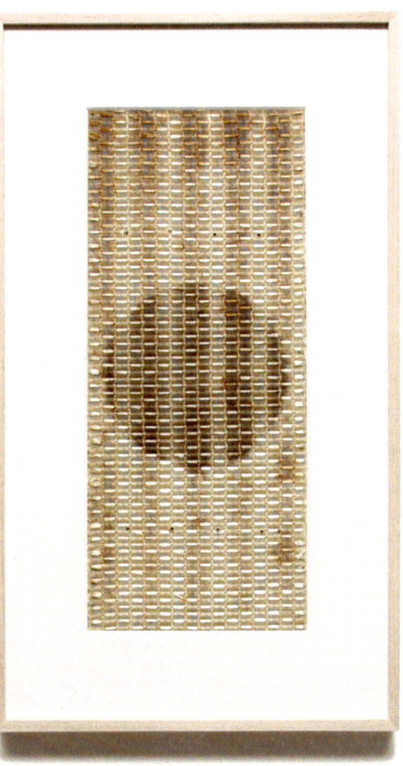

PL. 6
B-53, 2015

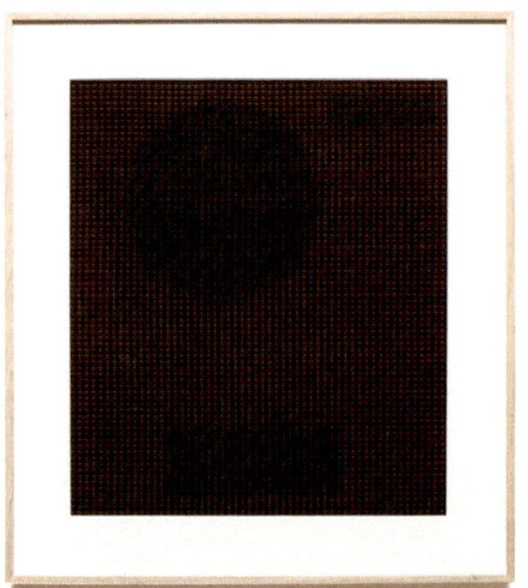

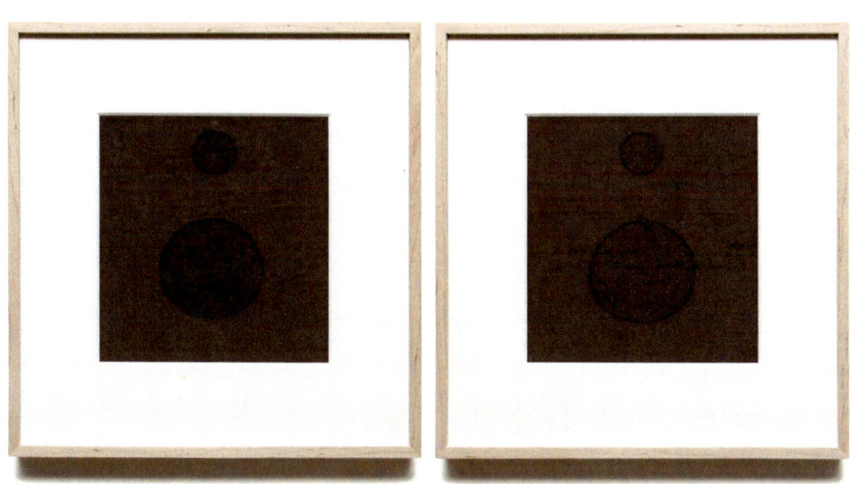

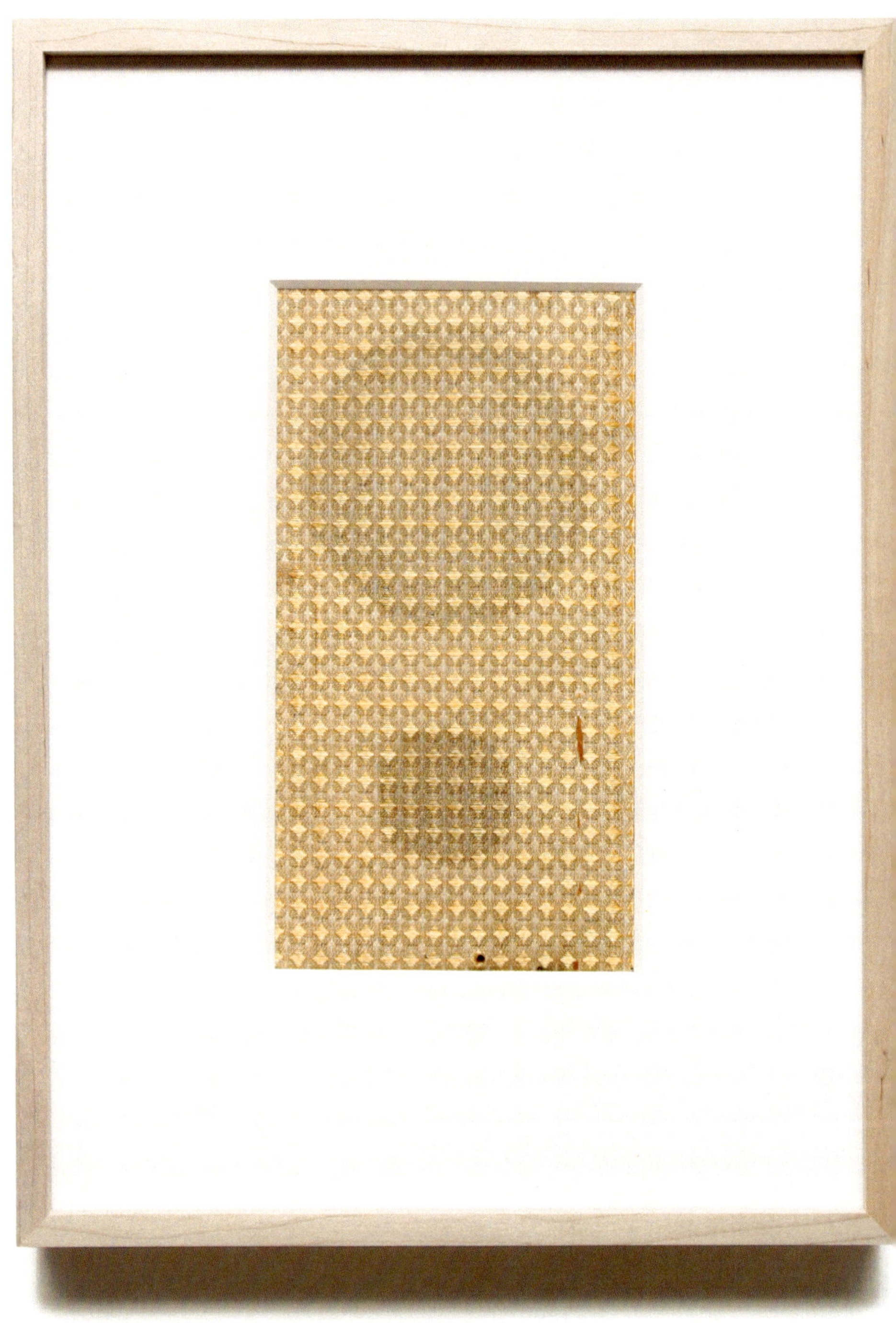

PL. 9
B-65, 2015

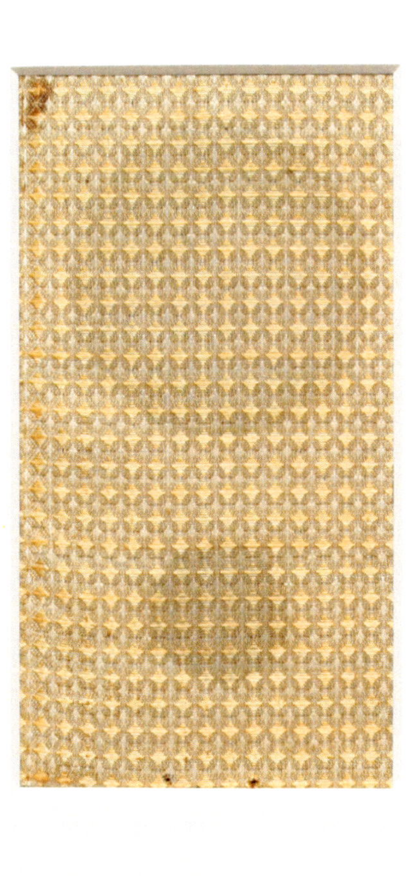

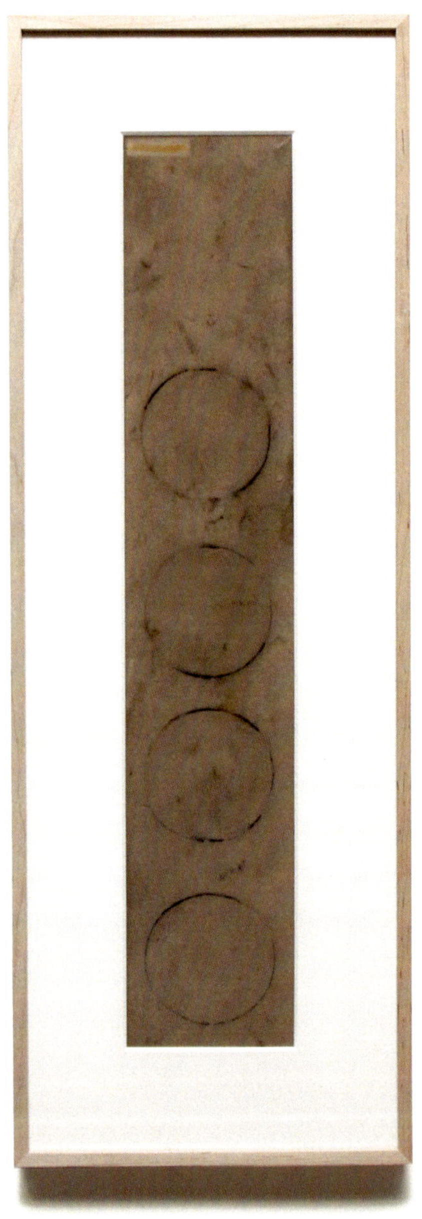 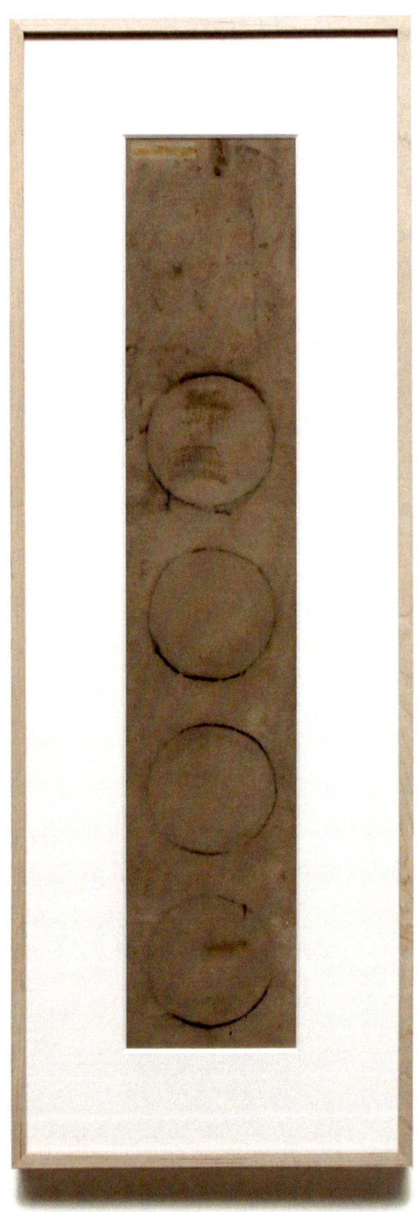

PL. 10
B-66, 2015

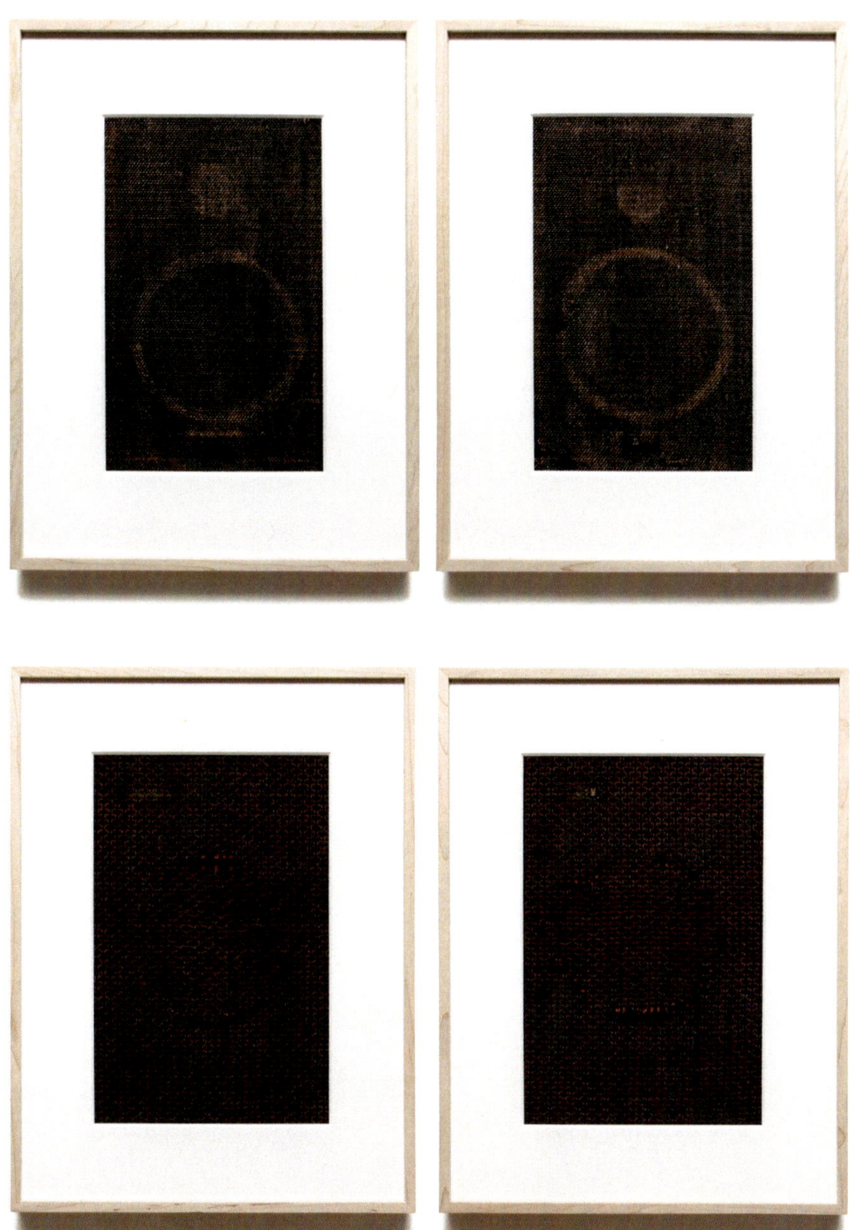

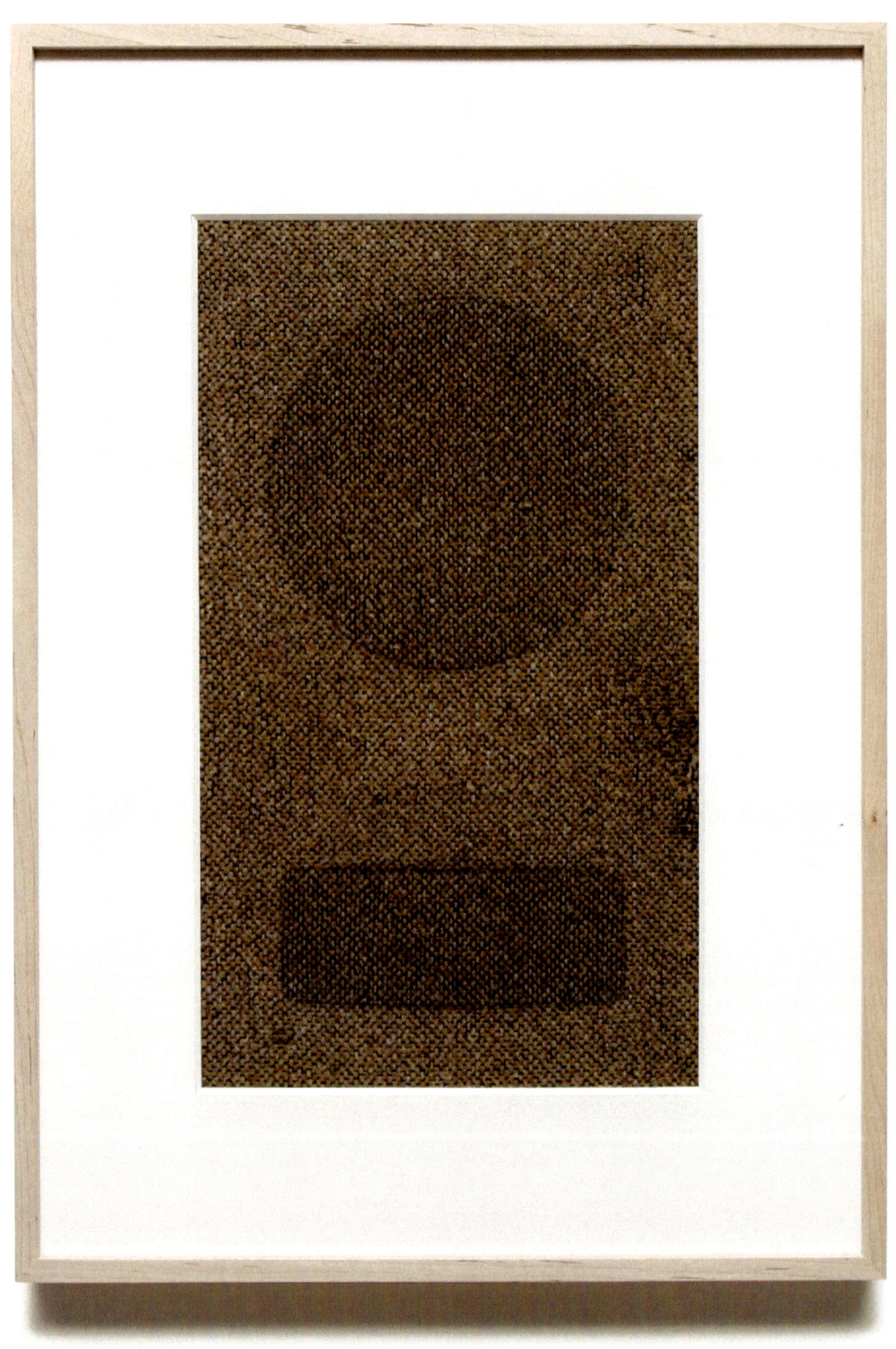

PL. 13
B-70, 2015

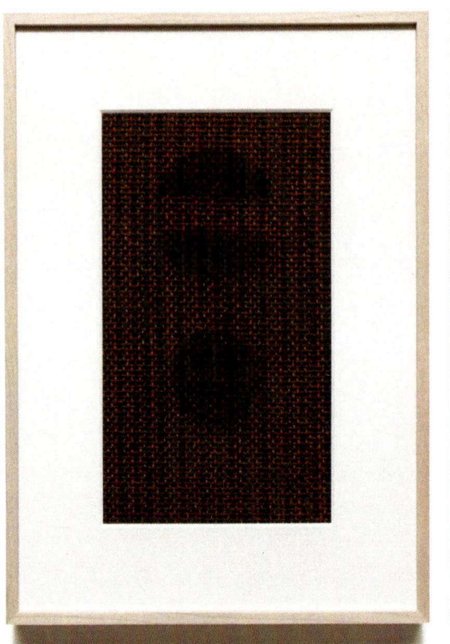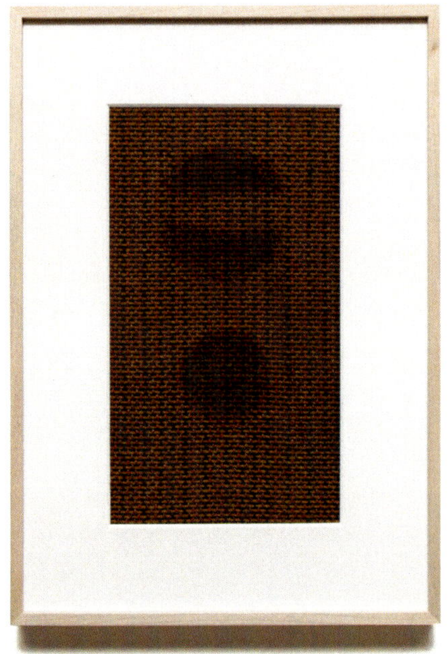

PL. 14
B-71, 2015

PL. 15
B-74, 2015

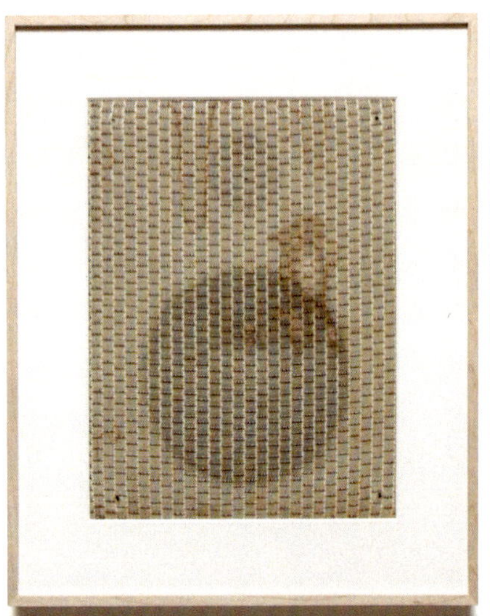 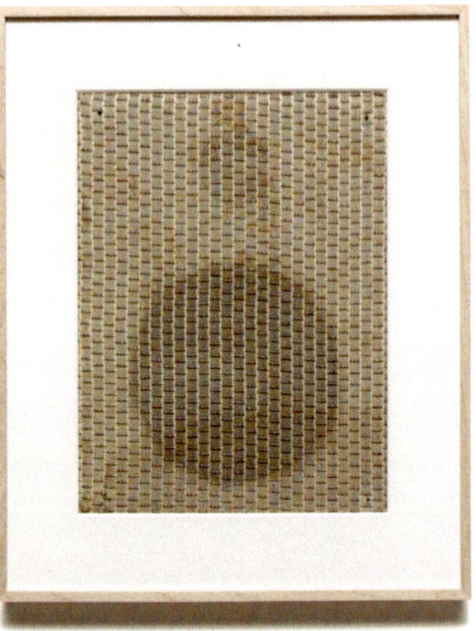

PL. 16
B-80, 2015

PL. 19
B-82, 2015

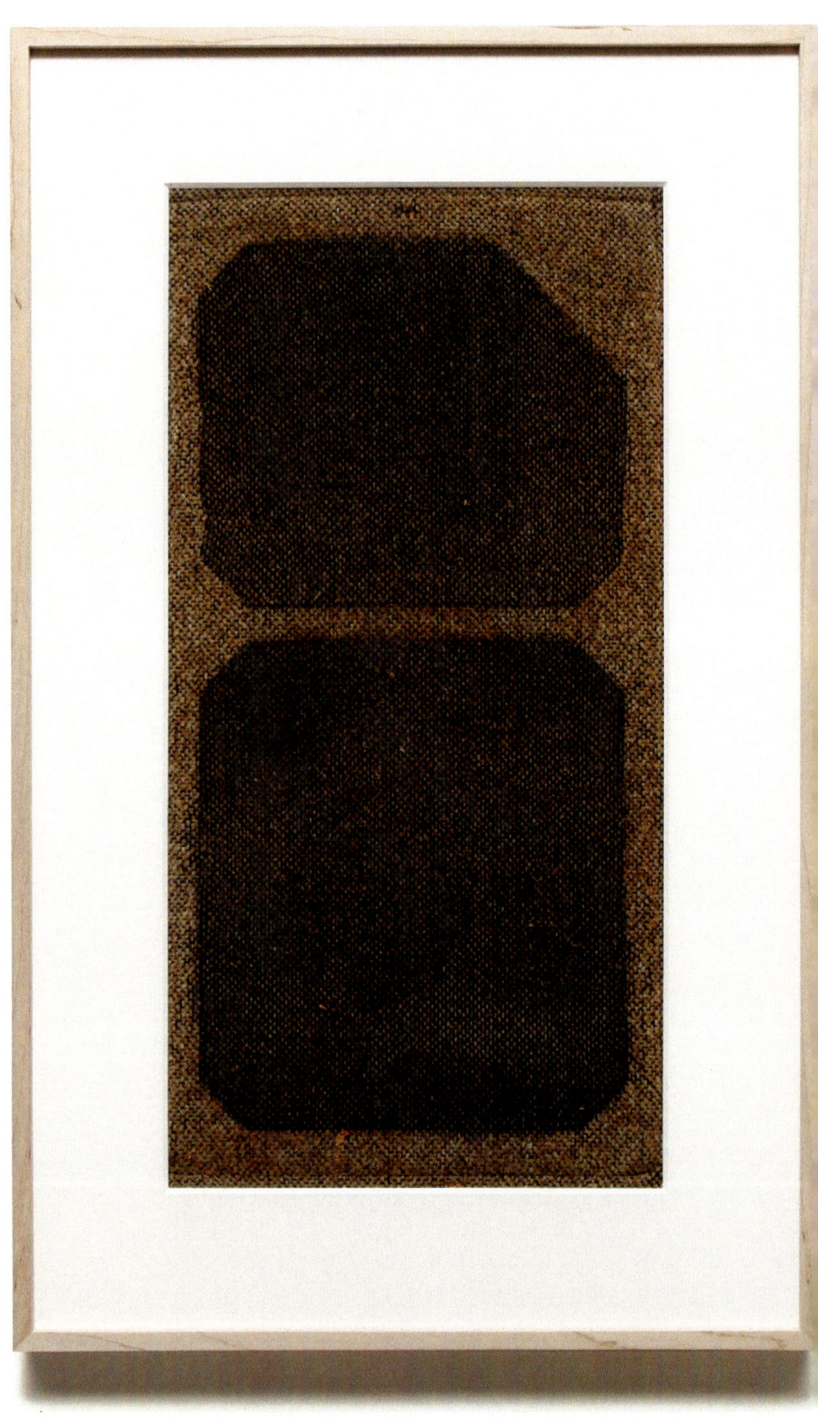

PL. 20
B-83, 2015

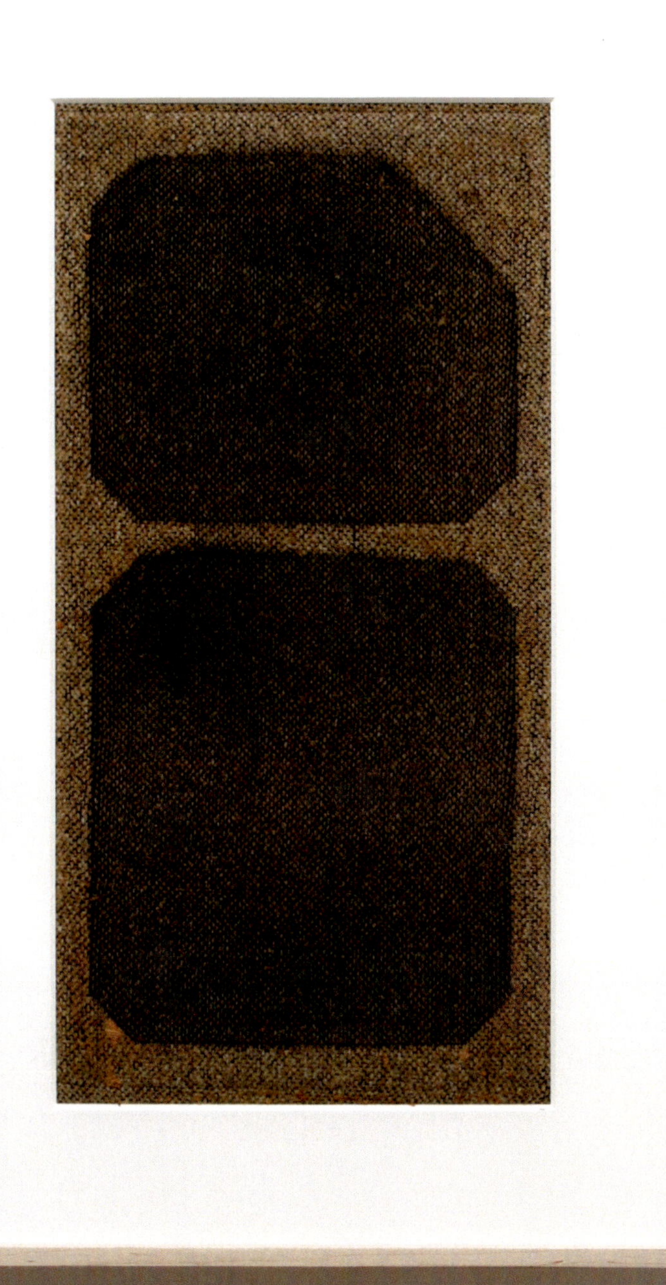

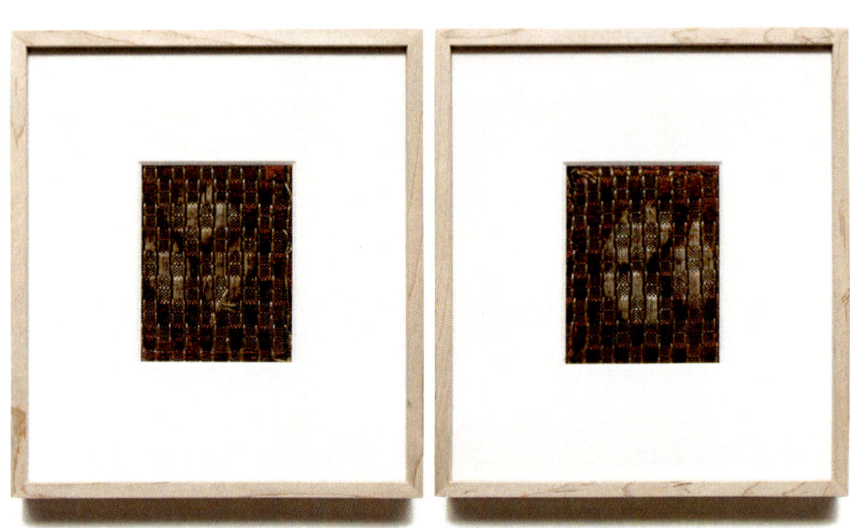

PL. 21
B-84, 2015

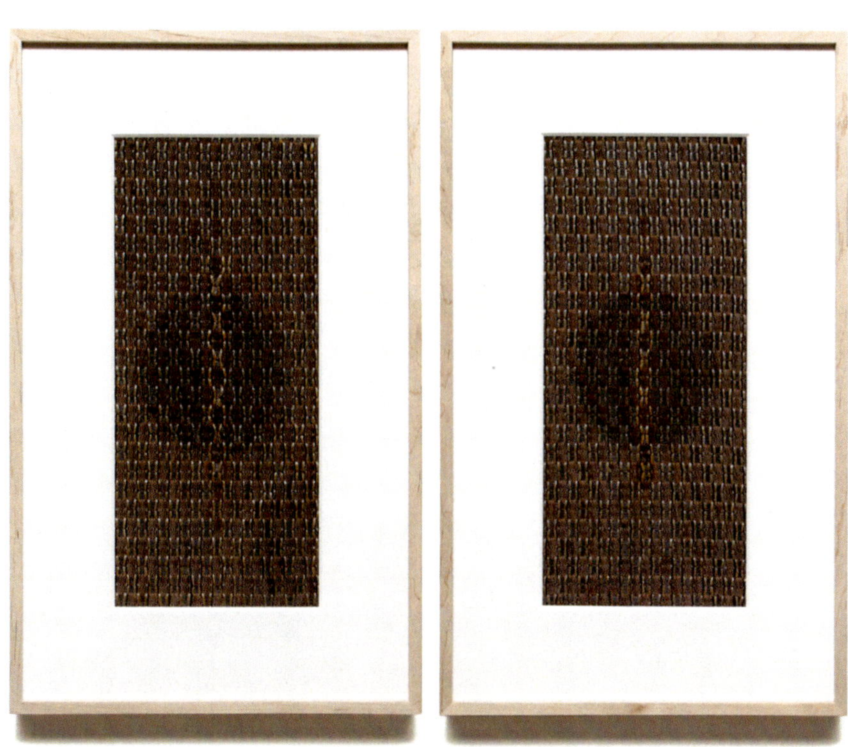

PL. 23
B-87, 2015

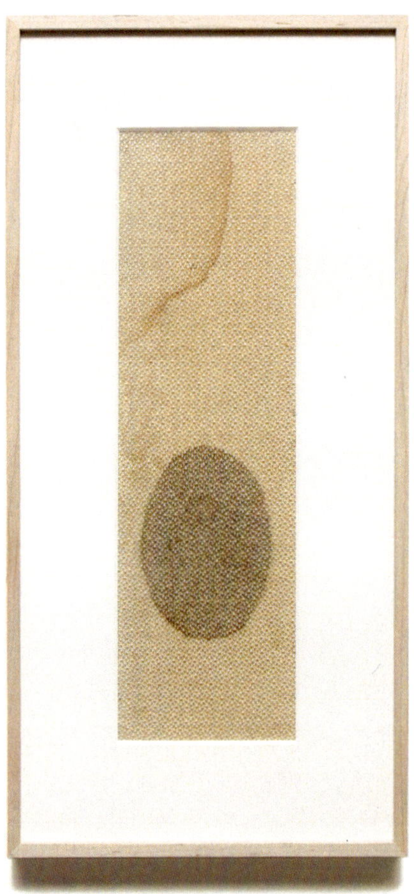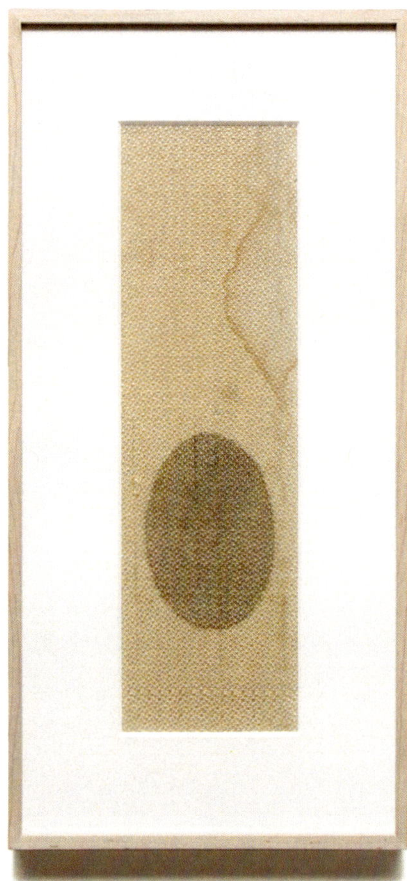

PL. 24
B-101, 2015

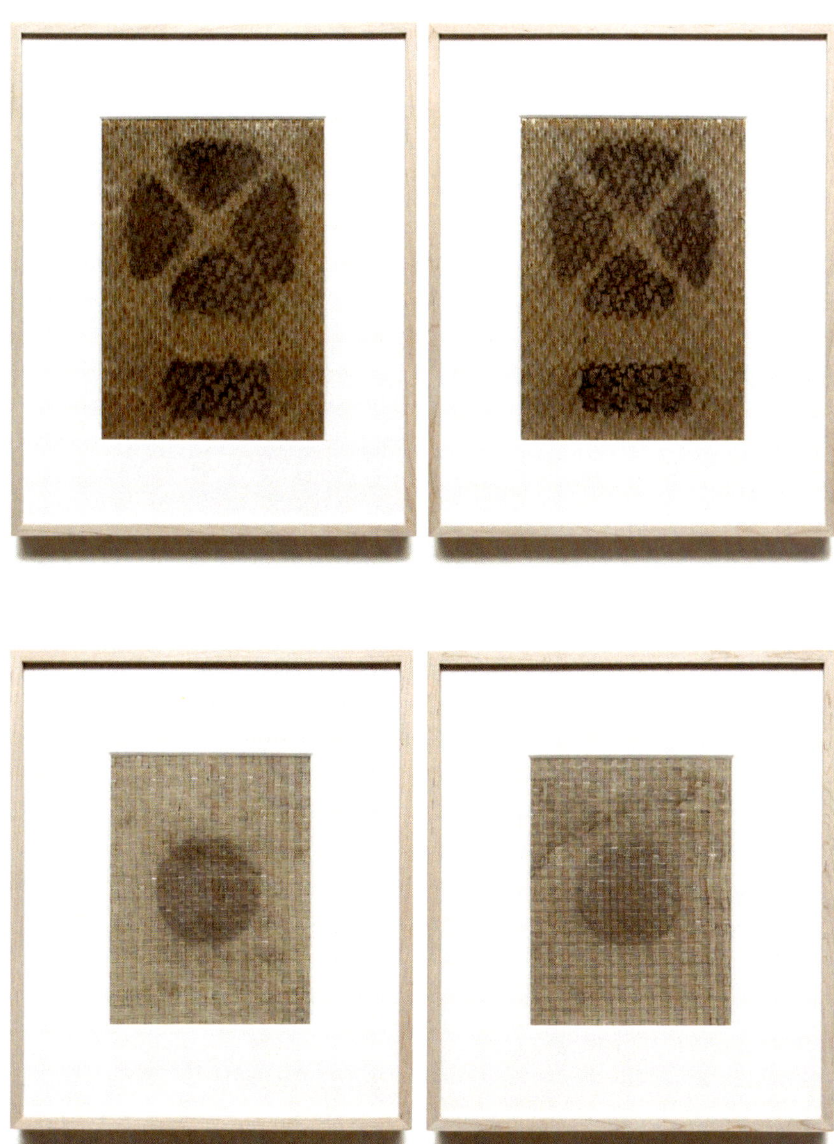

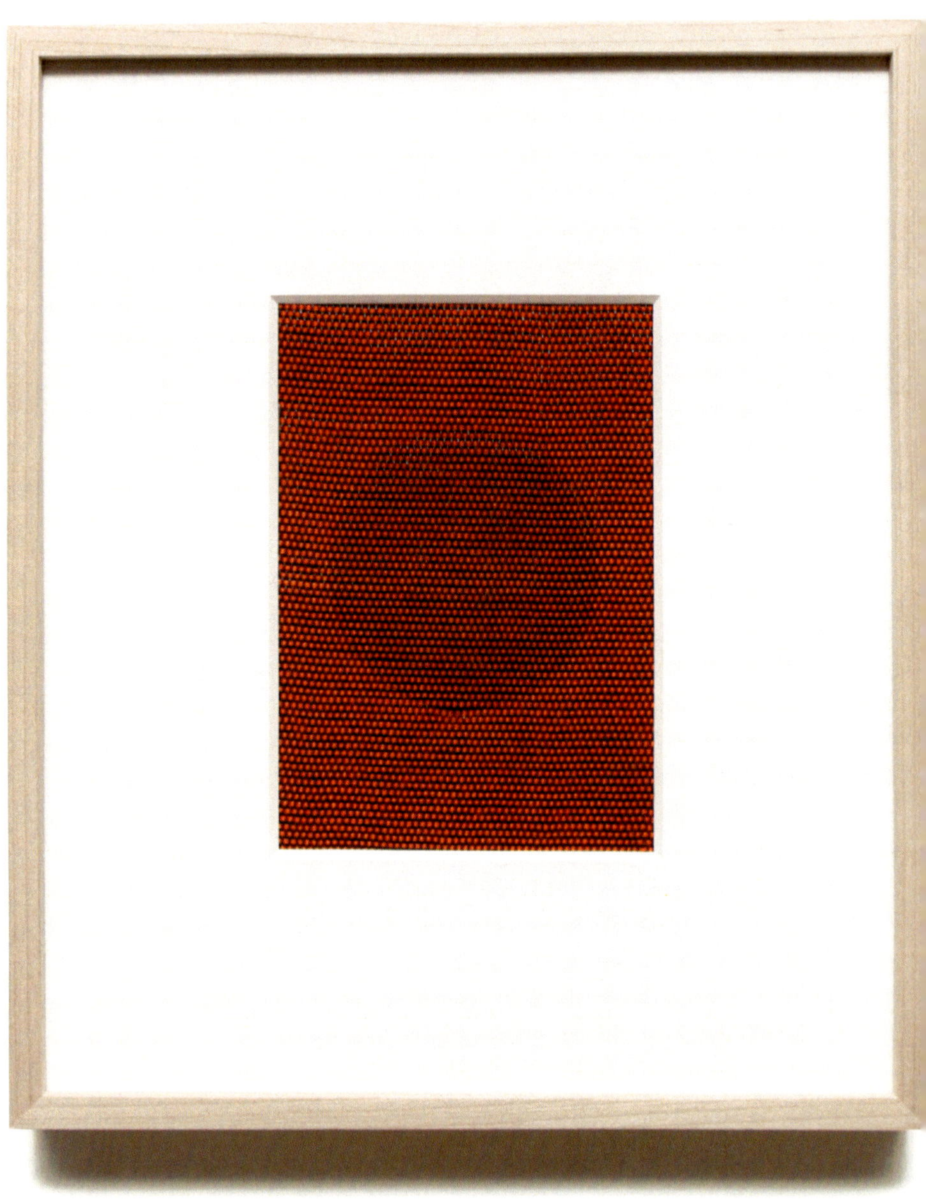

PL. 27
B-135, 2015

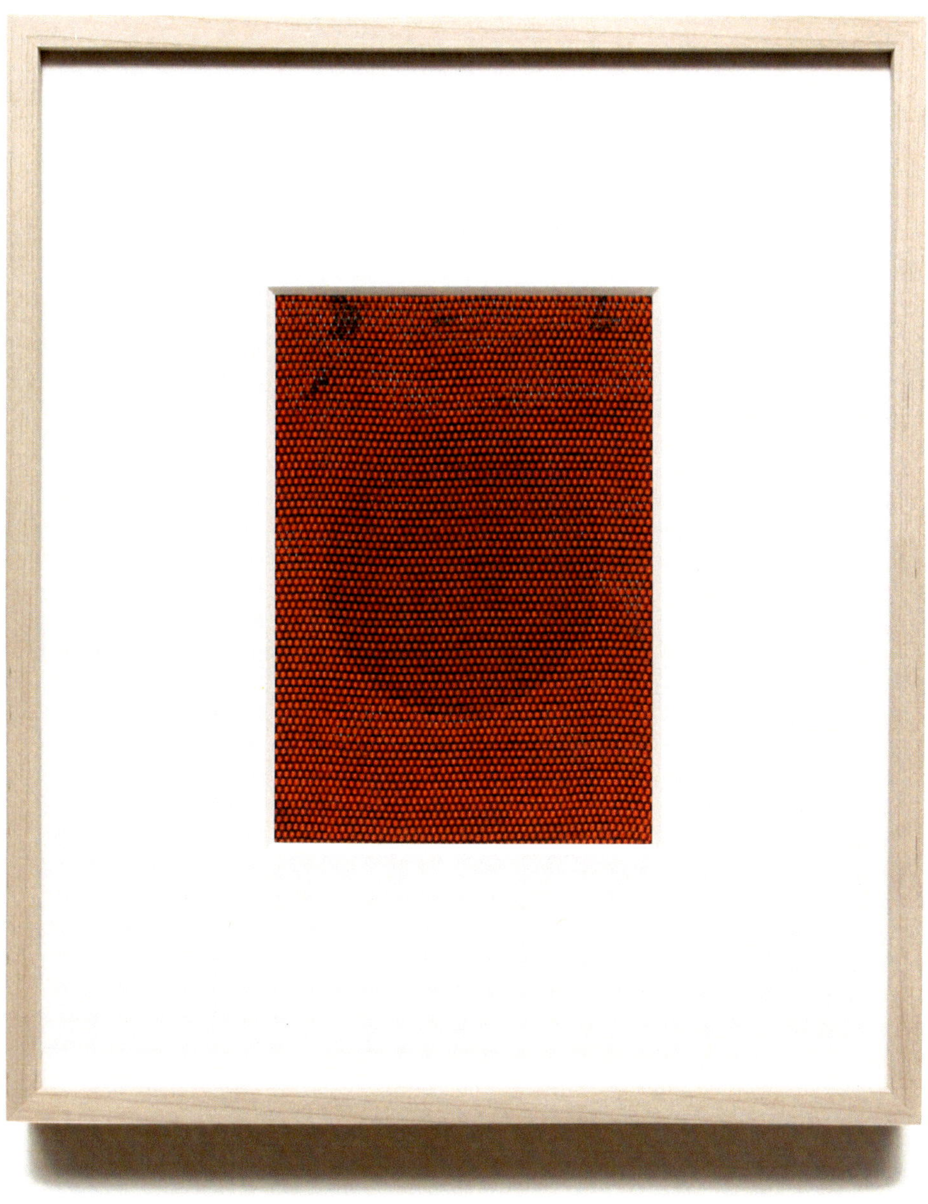

PL. 28
B-136, 2015

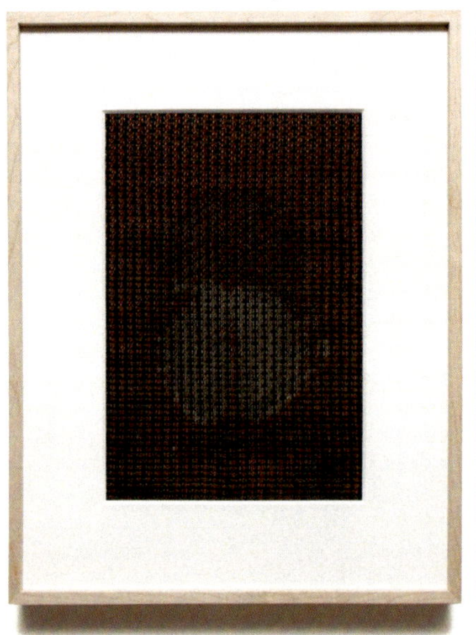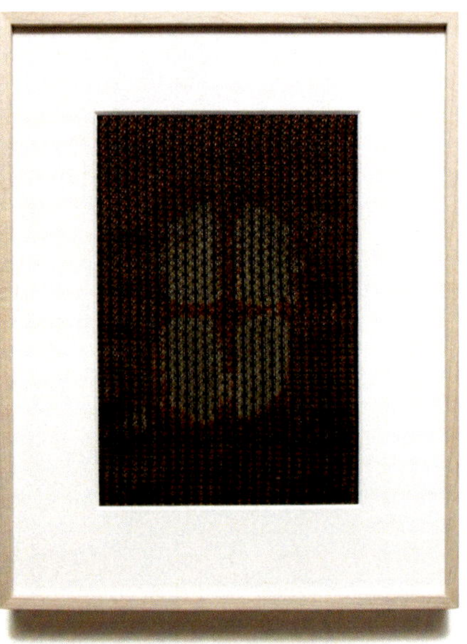

PL. 29
B-137, 2015

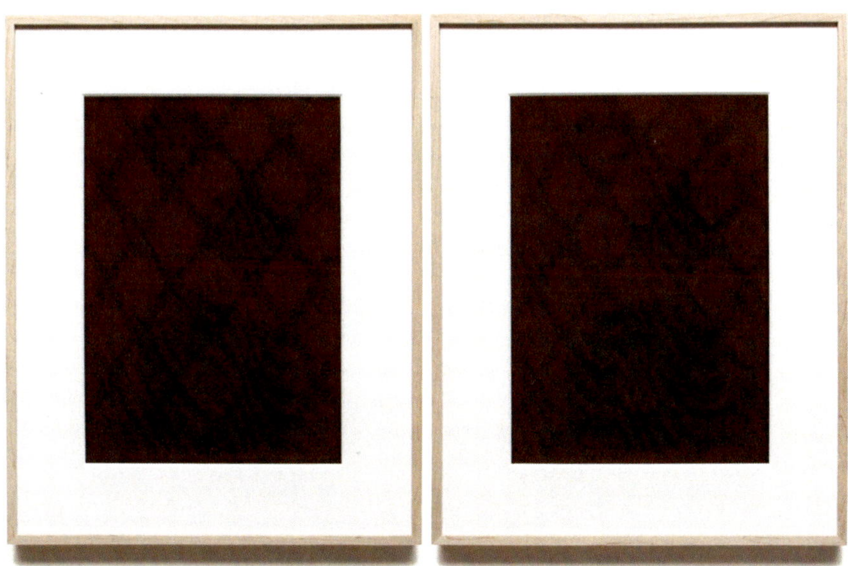

PL. 30
B-140, 2015

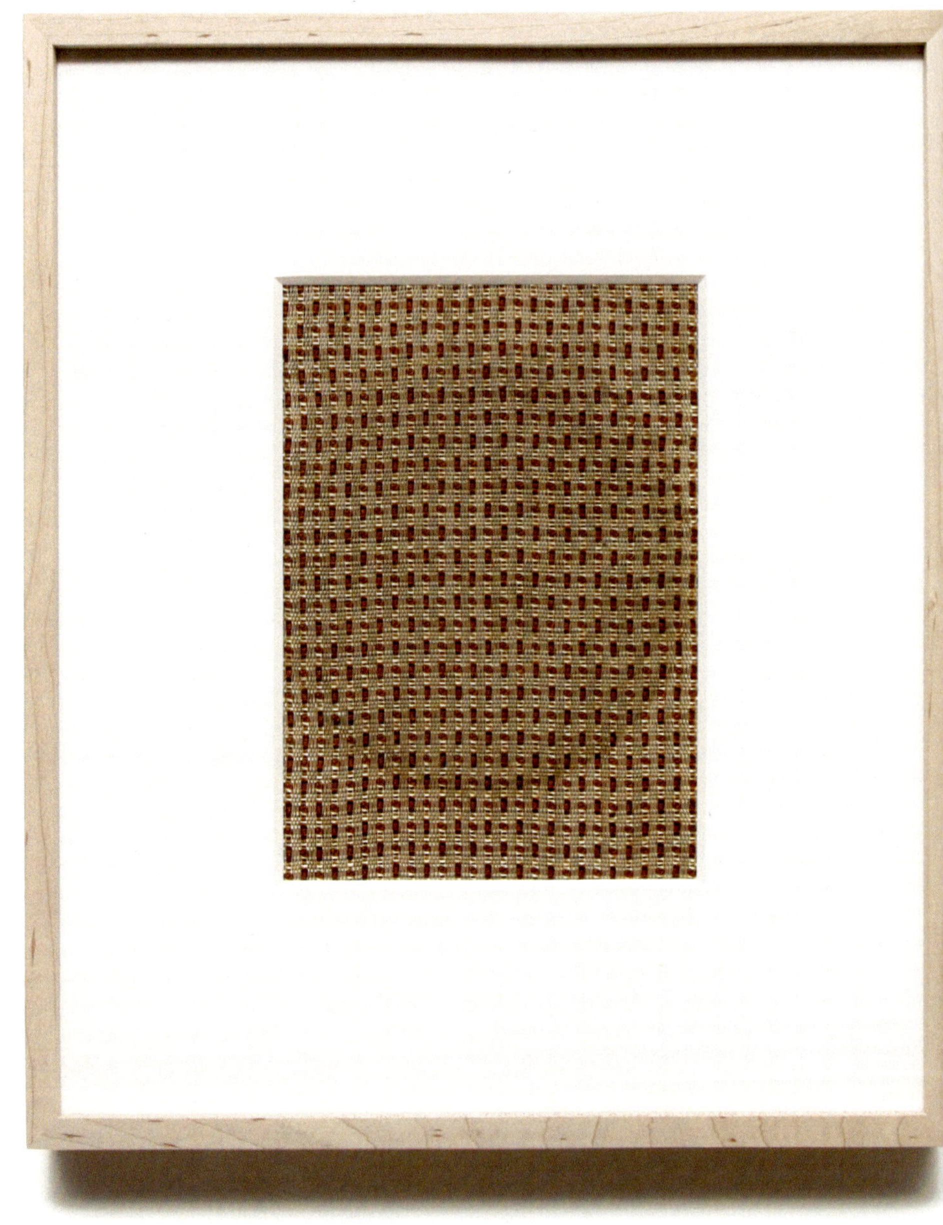

PL. 31
B-141, 2015

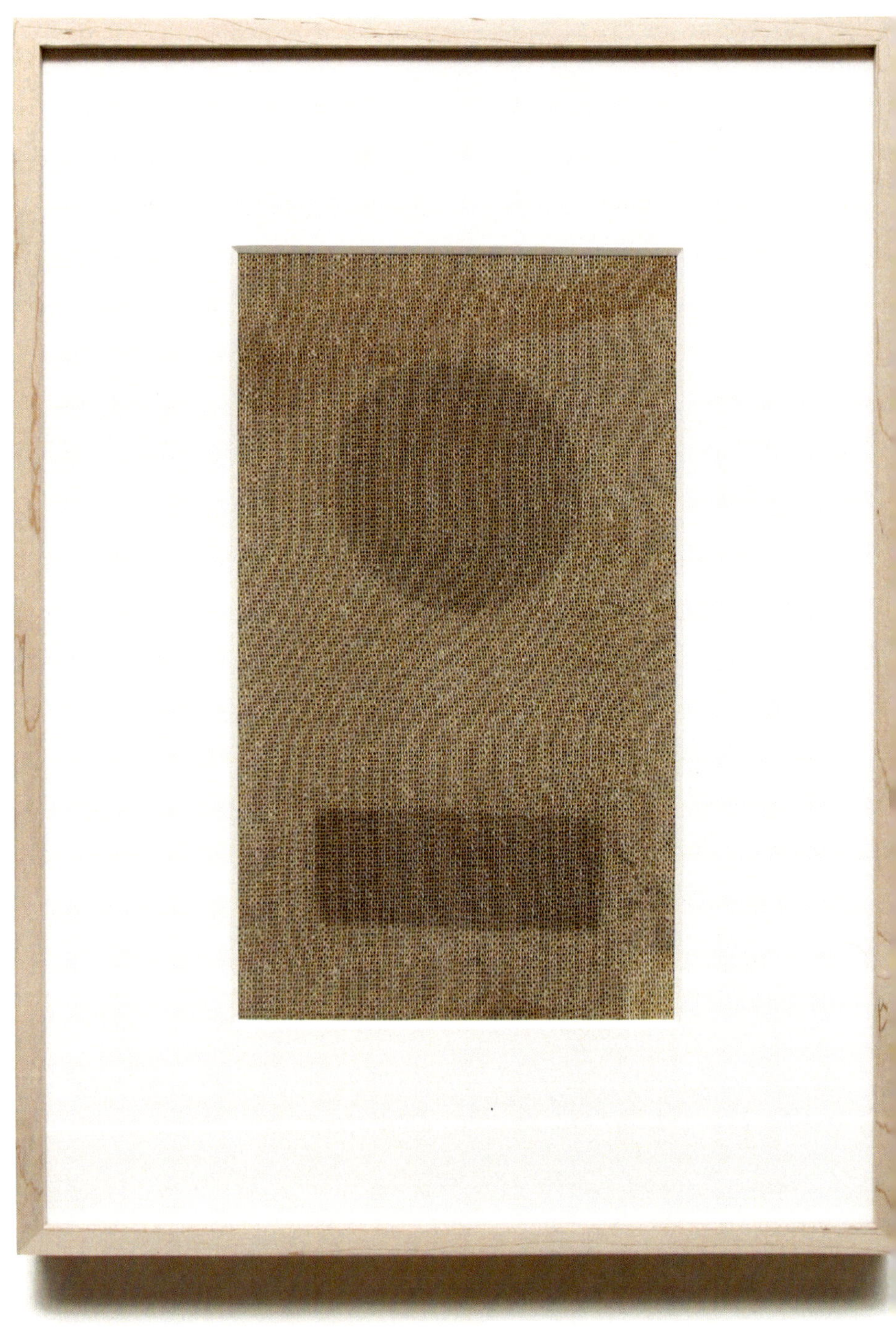

PL. 32
B-142, 2015

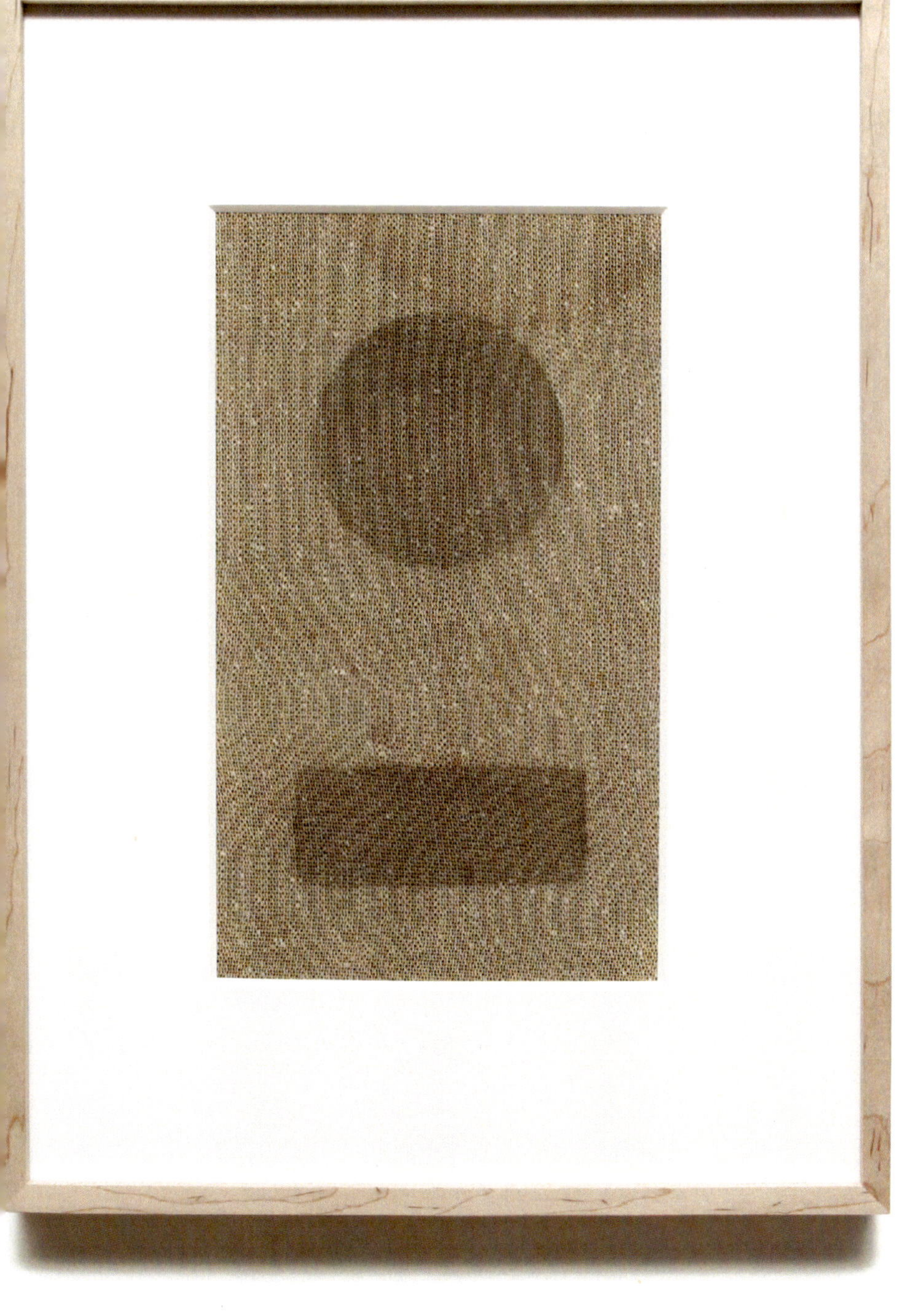

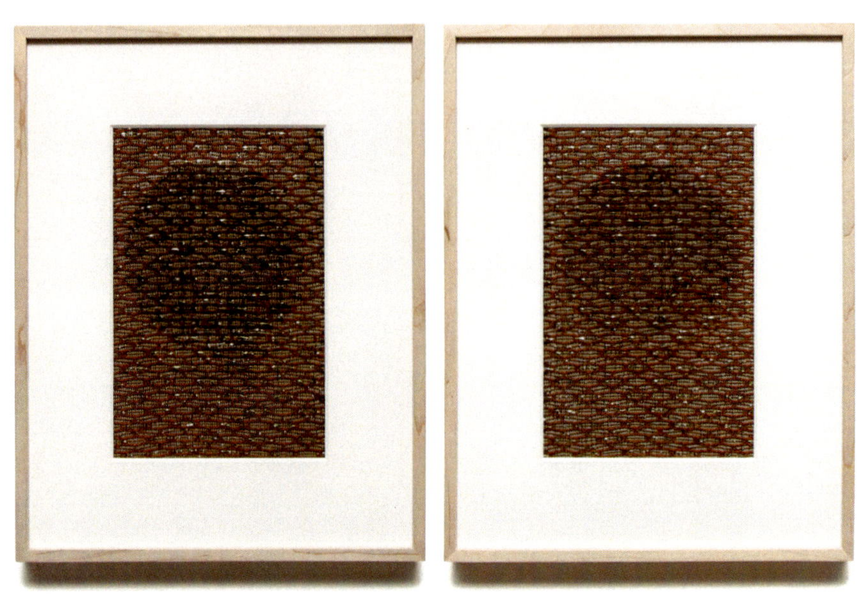

PL. 33
B-143, 2015

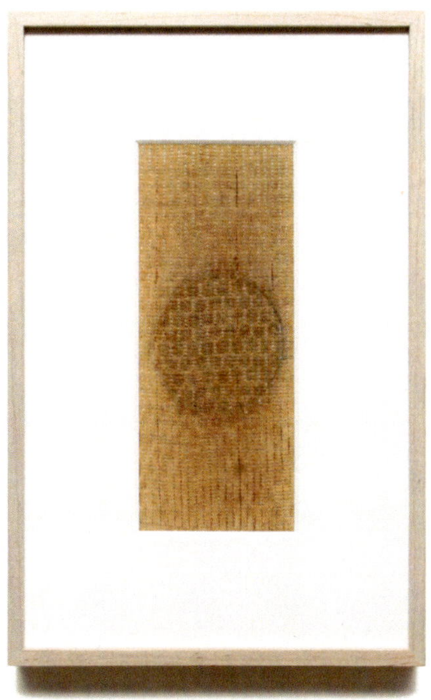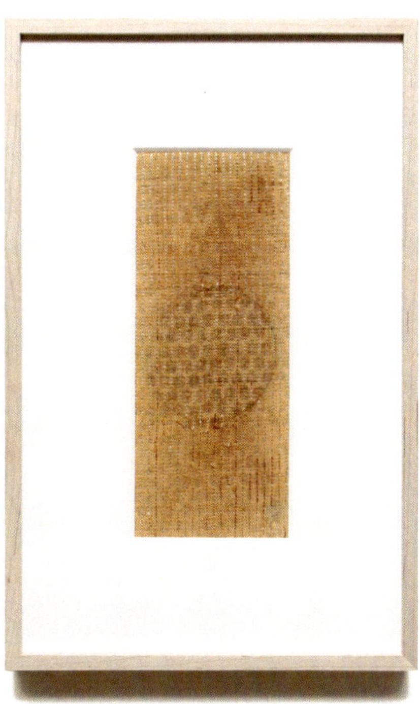

PL. 34
B-145, 2015

PL. 36
B-151, 2015

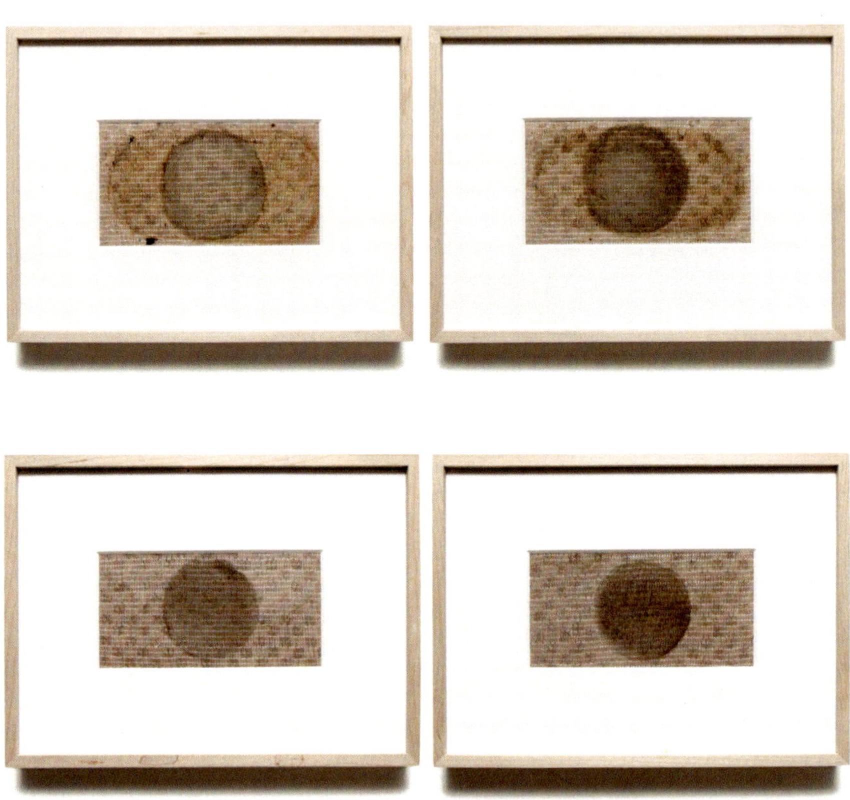

PL. 37 / PL. 38
B-170, 2015 / *B-178*, 2015

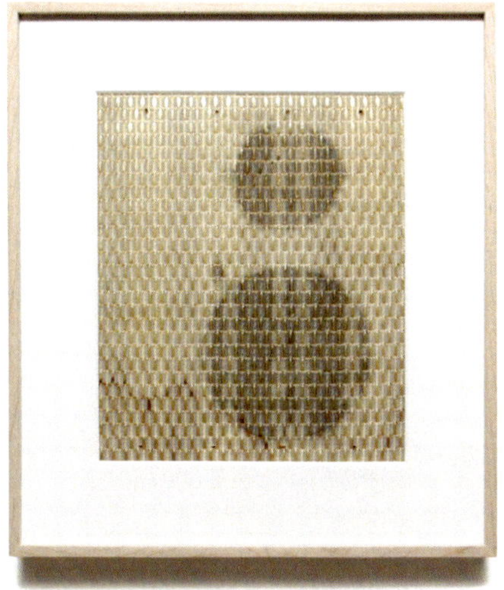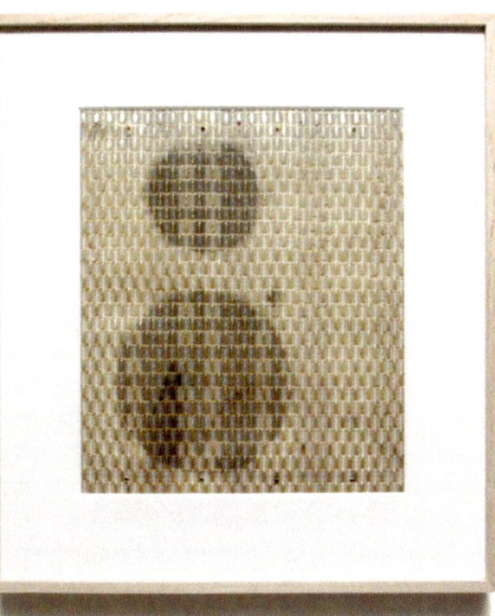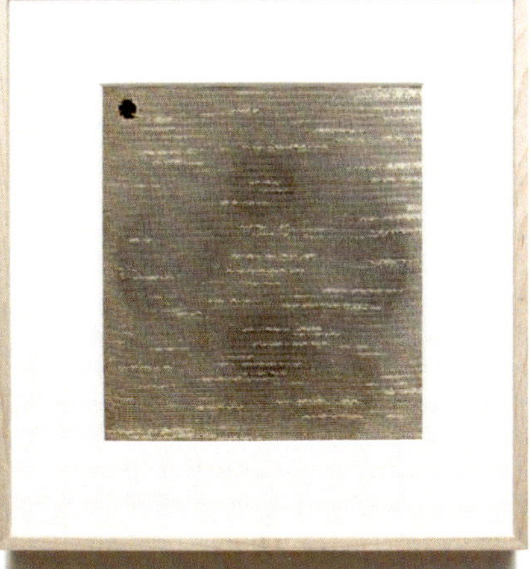

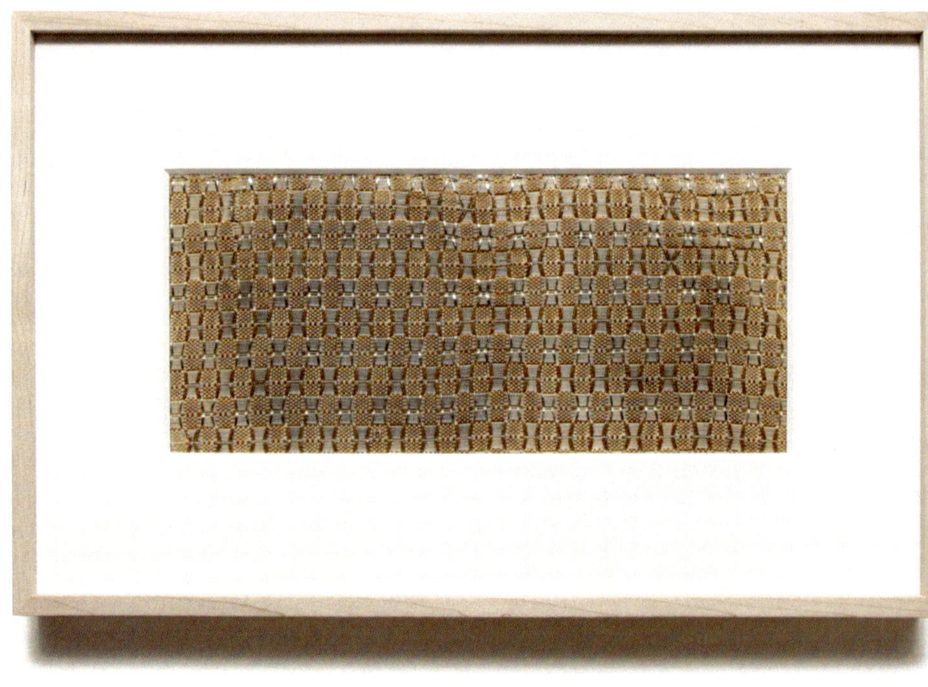

PL. 41
B-181, 2015

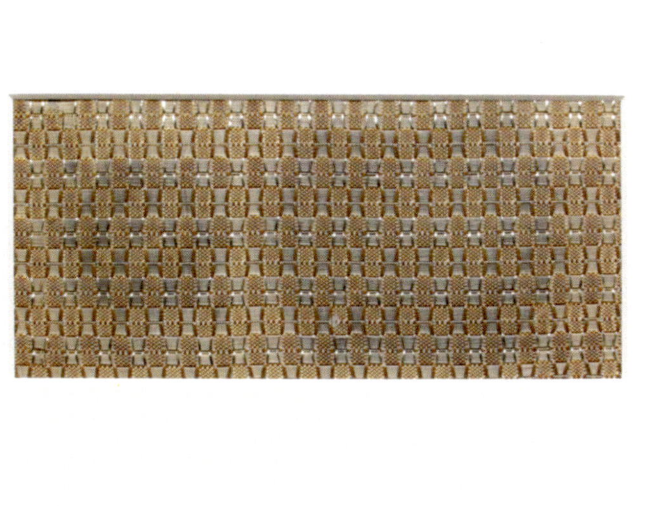

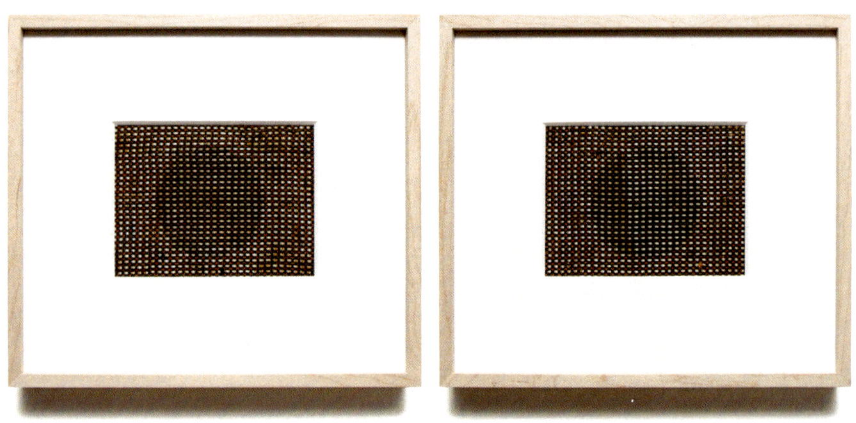

PL. 42
B-183, 2015

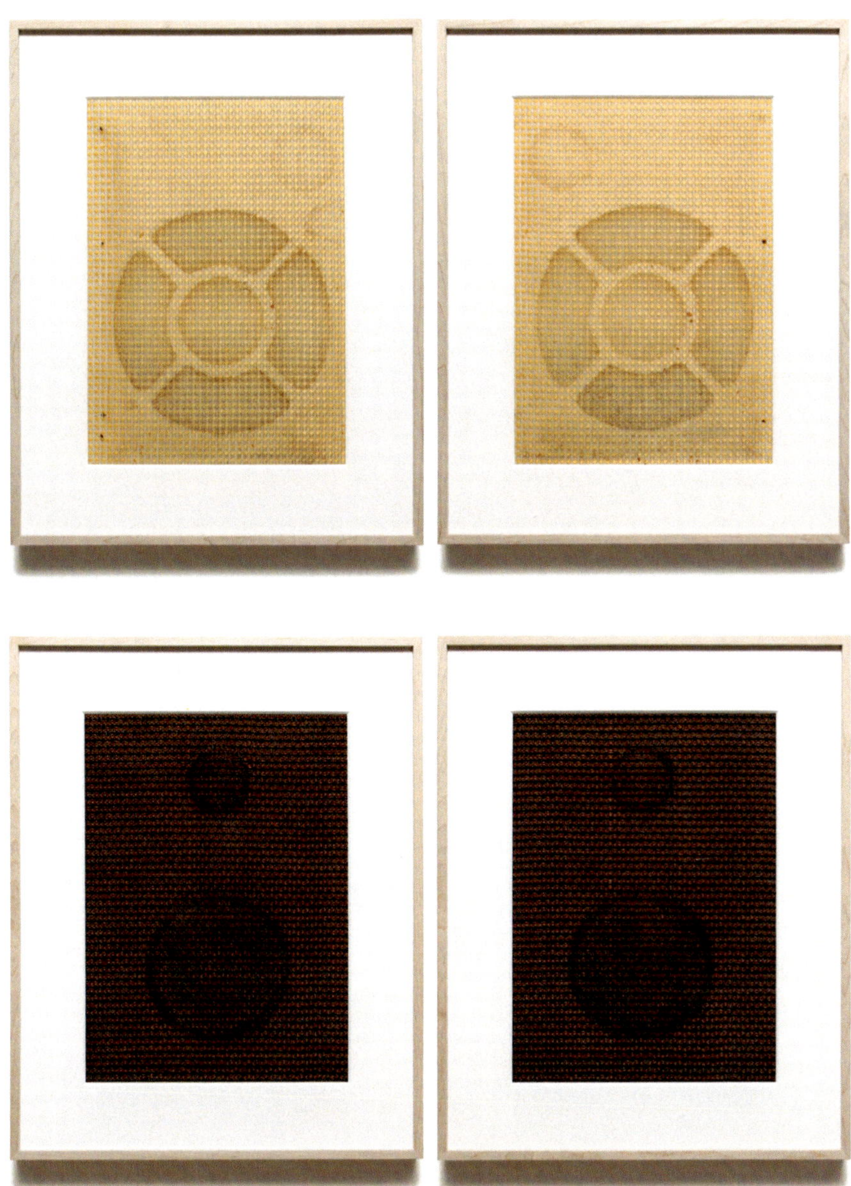

PL. 43 / PL. 44
B-189, 2015 / *B-182*, 2015

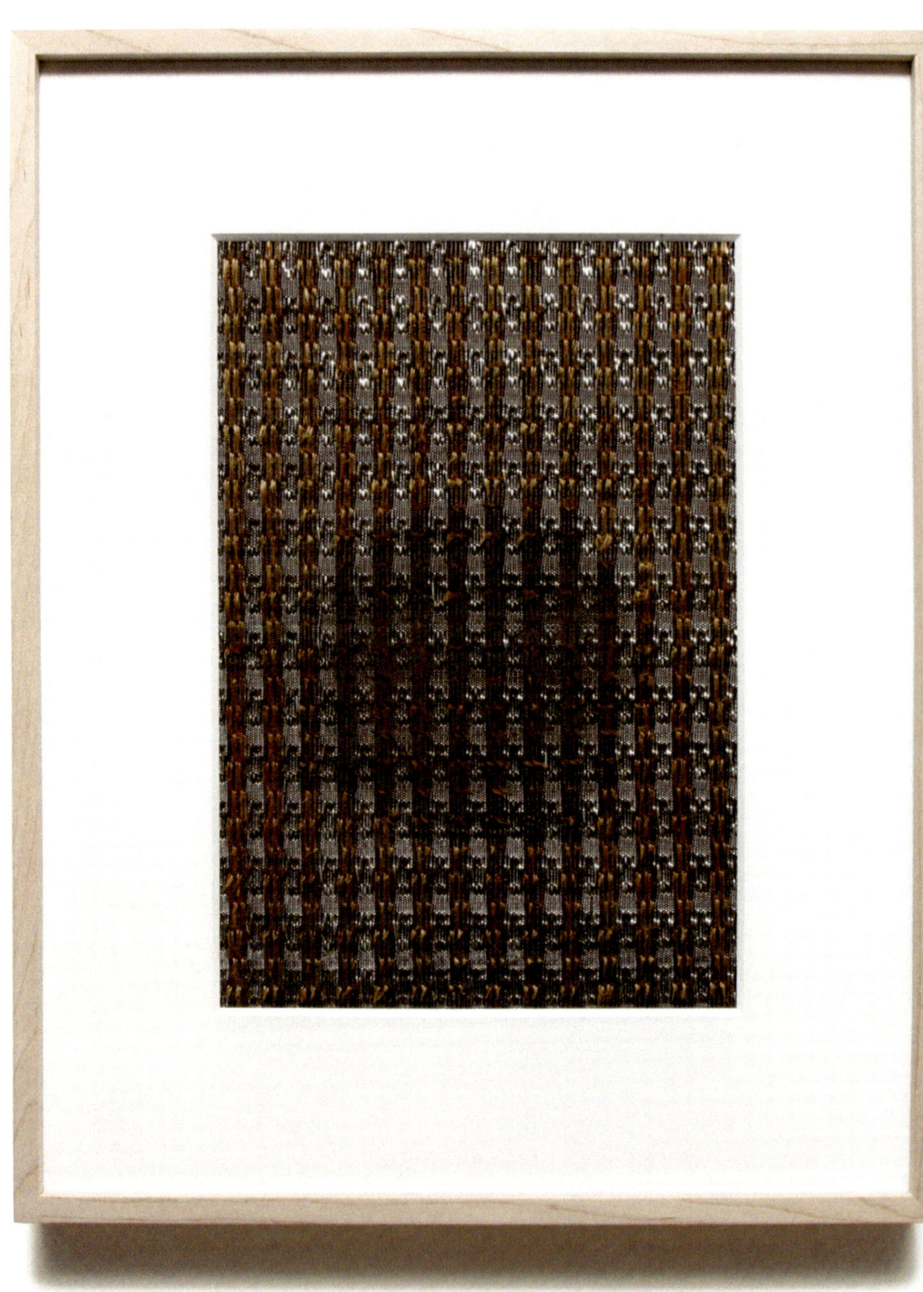

PL. 45
B-194, 2015

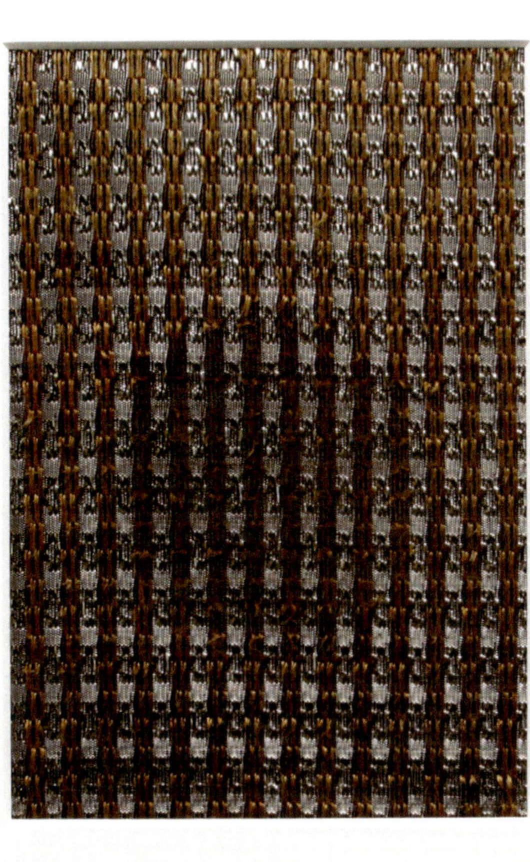

PL. 46
B-195, 2015

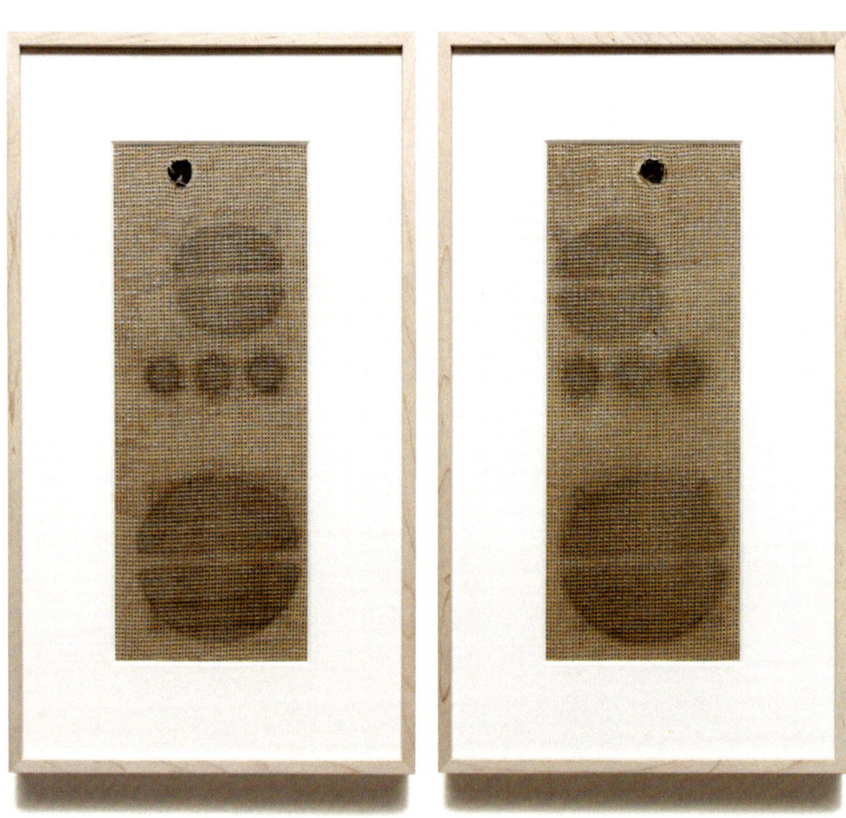

PL. 47
B-196, 2015

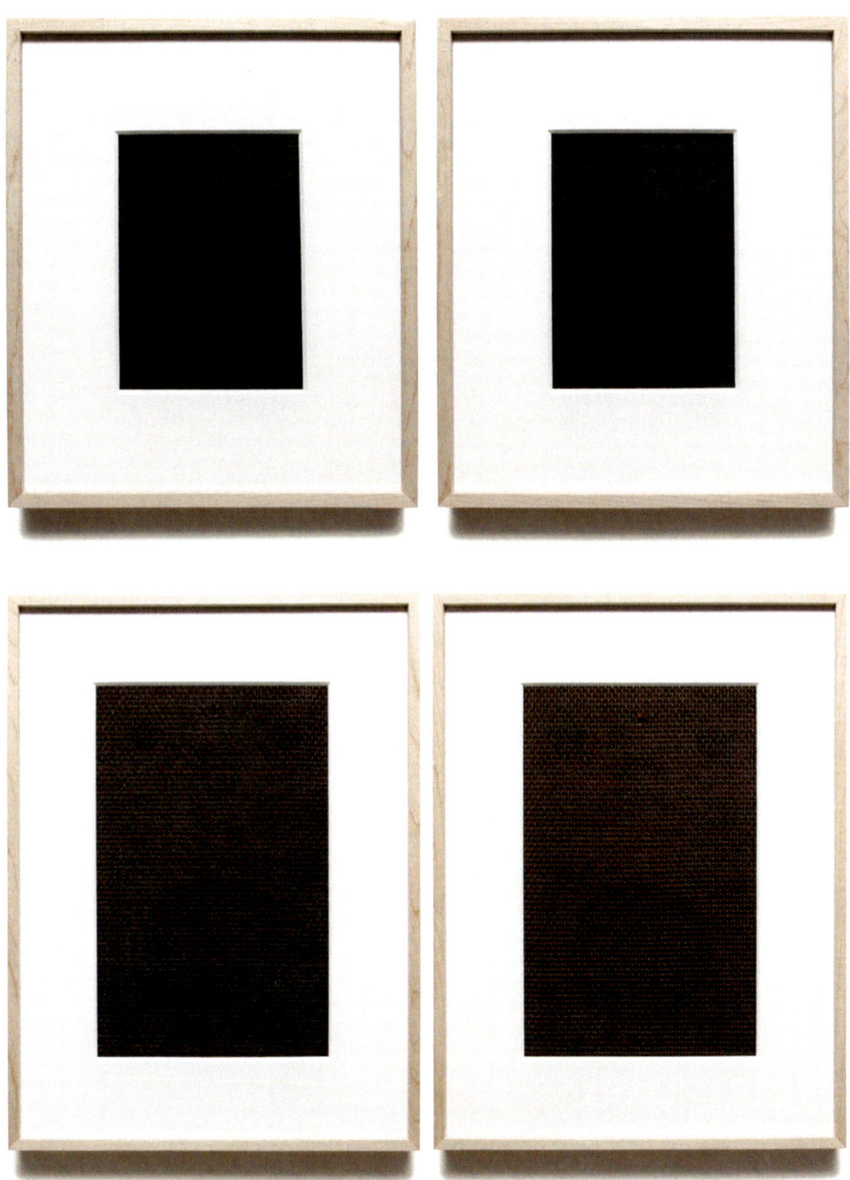

PL. 48 / PL. 49
B-208, 2015 / B-210, 2015

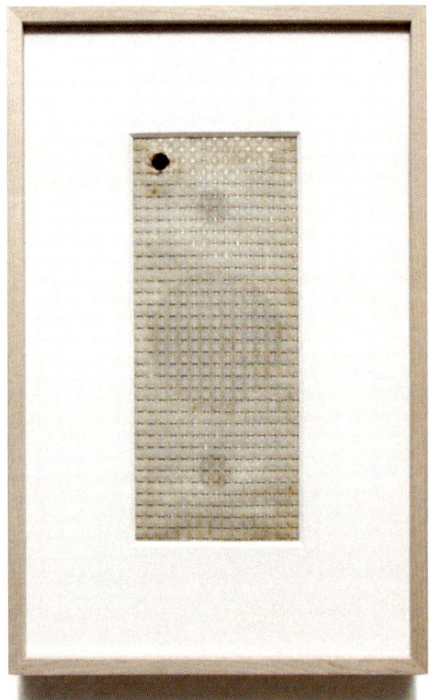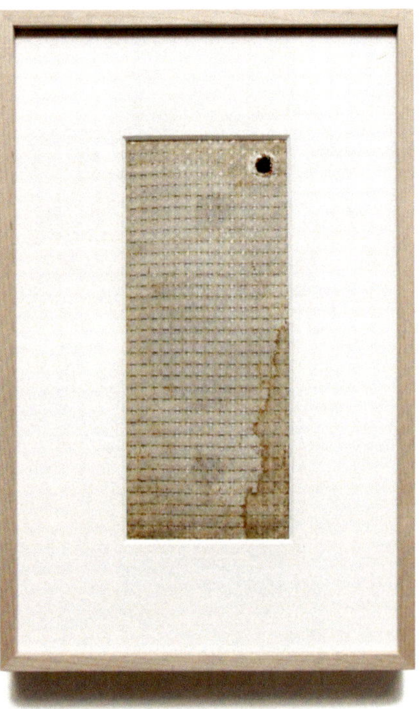

PL. 50
B-235, 2015

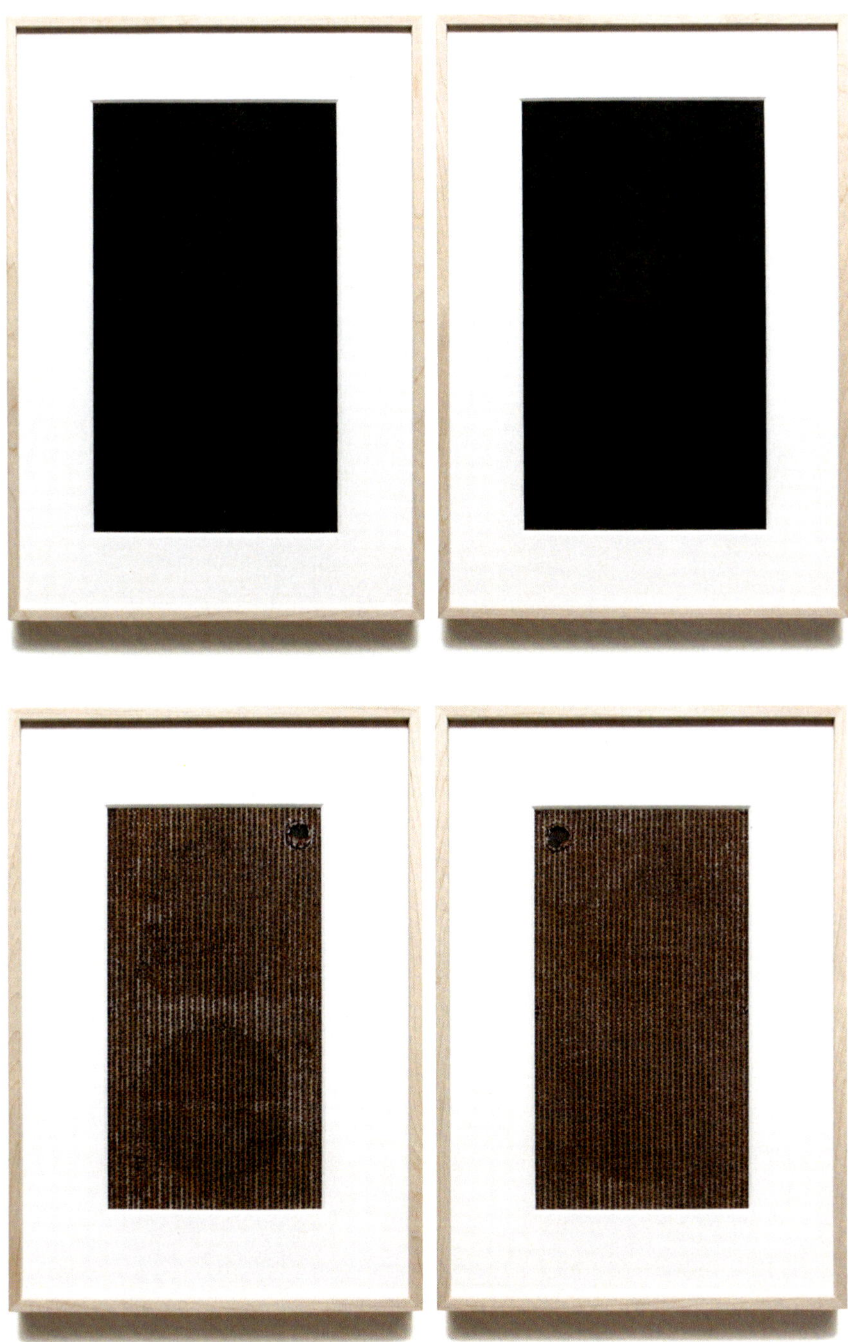

PL. 51 / PL. 52
B-252, 2015 / B-310, 2015

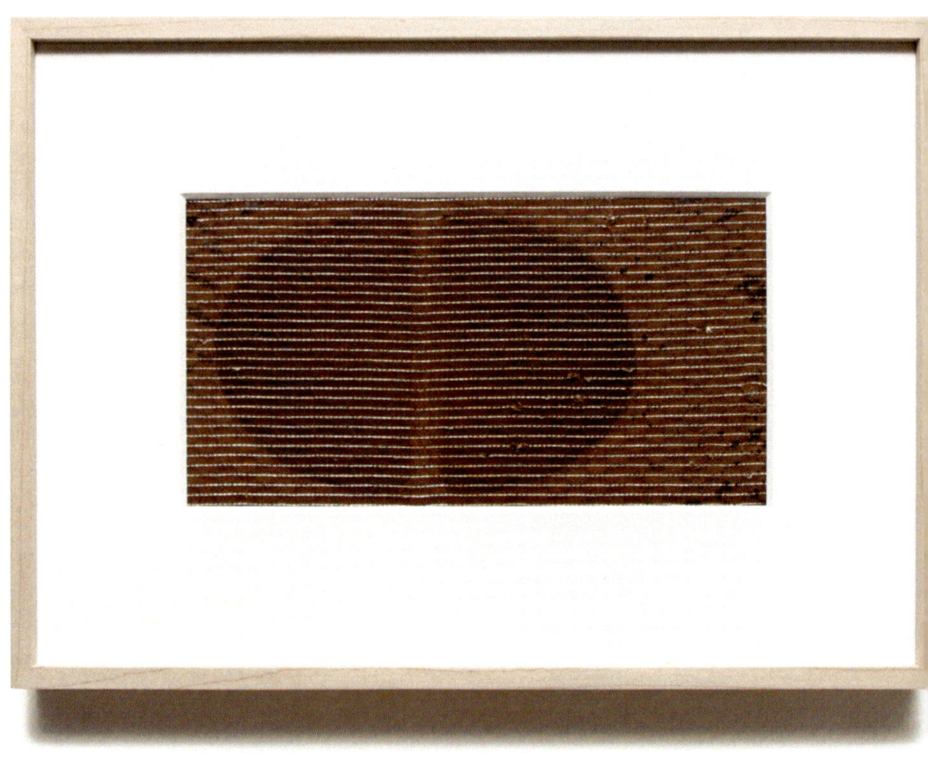

PL. 53
B-288, 2015

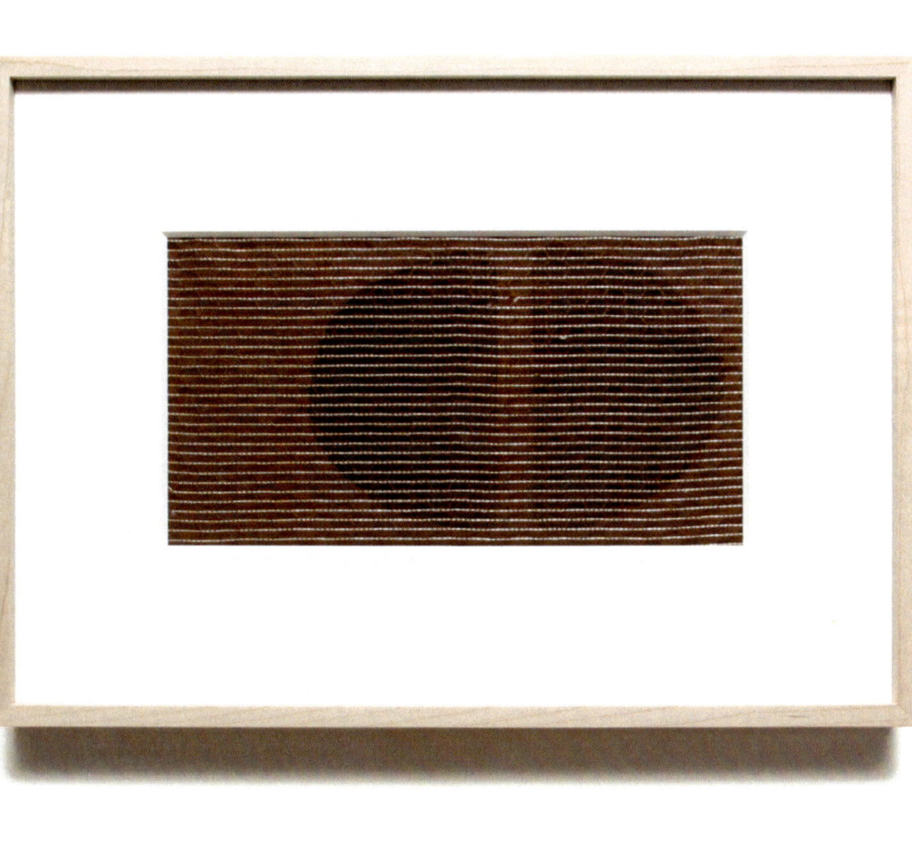

B-315, 2015

PL. 55
B-321, 2015

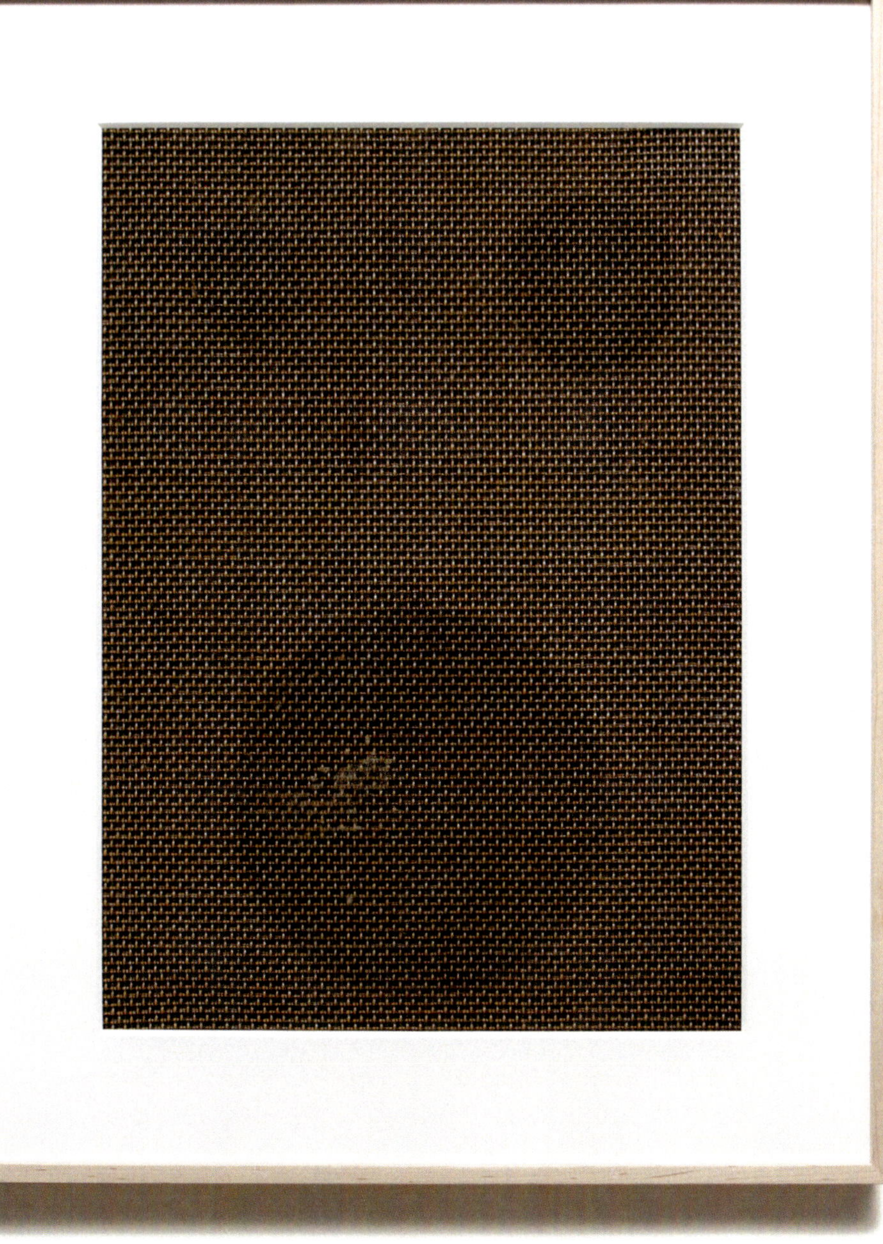

All works courtesy of
Timothy Taylor, London,
Proyectos Monclova, Mexico City, and
Sicardi Gallery, Houston.

PL. 1
B-17, 2015
Vintage radio speaker fabric
11 1/2 x 5 3/4 inches each

PL. 2
B-32, 2015
Vintage radio speaker fabric
4 1/2 x 4 3/8 inches each

PL. 3
B-31, 2015
Vintage radio speaker fabric
7 3/4 x 6 inches each

PL. 4
B-37, 2015
Vintage radio speaker fabric
5 1/2 x 23 3/4 inches each

PL. 5
B-39, 2015
Vintage radio speaker fabric
14 7/8 x 12 5/8 inches each

PL. 6
B-53, 2015
Vintage radio speaker fabric
19 3/4 x 8 1/2 inches each

PL. 7
B-62, 2015
Vintage radio speaker fabric
24 1/8 x 21 1/2 inches each

PL. 8
B-64, 2015
Vintage radio speaker fabric
9 7/8 x 9 1/2 inches each

PL. 9
B-65, 2015
Vintage radio speaker fabric
9 1/2 x 5 1/8 inches each

PL. 10
B-66, 2015
Vintage radio speaker fabric
28 7/8 x 5 1/2 inches each

PL. 11
B-68, 2015
Vintage radio speaker fabric
13 3/8 x 8 1/2 inches each

PL. 12
B-69, 2015
Vintage radio speaker fabric
15 7/8 x 10 3/8 inches each

PL. 13
B-70, 2015
Vintage radio speaker fabric
16 3/4 x 9 7/8 inches each

PL. 14

B-71, 2015

Vintage radio speaker fabric

15 3/8 x 8 7/8 inches each

PL. 15

B-74, 2015

Vintage radio speaker fabric

11 7/8 x 8 3/4 inches each

PL. 16

B-80, 2015

Vintage radio speaker fabric

18 1/4 x 13 7/8 inches each

PL. 17

B-81, 2015

Vintage radio speaker fabric

16 1/4 x 7 1/2 inches each

PL. 18

B-79, 2015

Vintage radio speaker fabric

19 x 13 3/8 inches each

PL. 19

B-82, 2015

Vintage radio speaker fabric

21 5/8 x 13 1/8 inches each

PL. 20

B-83, 2015

Vintage radio speaker fabric

23 1/4 x 11 7/8 inches each

PL. 21

B-84, 2015

Vintage radio speaker fabric

5 5/8 x 4 3/8 inches each

PL. 22

B-85, 2015

Vintage radio speaker fabric

16 5/8 x 7 1/2 inches each

PL. 23

B-87, 2015

Vintage radio speaker fabric

22 7/8 x 10 1/4 inches each

PL. 24

B-101, 2015

Vintage radio speaker fabric

19 3/4 x 6 inches each

PL. 25

B-91, 2015

Vintage radio speaker fabric

12 5/8 x 9 1/8 inches each

PL. 26

B-134, 2015

Vintage radio speaker fabric

9 1/2 x 7 1/4 inches each

PL. 27 / FRONT & BACK COVER

B-135, 2015

Vintage radio speaker fabric

7 1/4 x 5 1/8 inches each

PL. 28

B-136, 2015

Vintage radio speaker fabric

10 5/8 x 8 1/2 inches each

PL. 29

B-137, 2015

Vintage radio speaker fabric

14 1/4 x 9 5/8 inches each

PL. 30

B-140, 2015

Vintage radio speaker fabric

17 x 12 1/8 inches each

PL. 31

B-141, 2015

Vintage radio speaker fabric

8 3/8 x 6 inches each

PL. 32

B-142, 2015

Vintage radio speaker fabric

12 1/4 x 7 1/8 inches each

PL. 33

B-143, 2015

Vintage radio speaker fabric

12 1/8 x 7 7/8 inches each

PL. 34

B-145, 2015

Vintage radio speaker fabric

10 7/8 x 4 1/2 inches each

PL. 35

B-148, 2015

Vintage radio speaker fabric

7 1/2 x 4 7/8 inches each

PL. 36

B-151, 2015

Vintage radio speaker fabric

6 3/8 x 27 1/4 inches each

PL. 37

B-170, 2015

Vintage radio speaker fabric

5 1/8 x 6 7/8 inches each

PL. 38

B-178, 2015

Vintage radio speaker fabric

4 1/4 x 8 3/4 inches each

PL. 39

B-177, 2015

Vintage radio speaker fabric

14 5/8 x 12 1/2 inches each

PL. 40

B-174, 2015

Vintage radio speaker fabric

12 x 11 1/8 inches each

PL. 41

B-181, 2015

Vintage radio speaker fabric

11 5/8 x 8 1/4 inches each

PL. 42
B-183, 2015
Vintage radio speaker fabric
5 1/8 x 6 7/8 inches each

PL. 43
B-189, 2015
Vintage radio speaker fabric
17 3/8 x 12 5/8 inches each

PL. 44
B-182, 2015
Vintage radio speaker fabric
18 x 13 1/8 inches each

PL. 45
B-194, 2015
Vintage radio speaker fabric
13 3/8 x 9 1/4 inches each

PL. 46
B-195, 2015
Vintage radio speaker fabric
12 x 20 7/8 inches each

PL. 47
B-196, 2015
Vintage radio speaker fabric
17 3/8 x 6 3/4 inches each

PL. 48
B-208, 2015
Vintage radio speaker fabric
8 1/8 x 5 7/8 inches each

PL. 49
B-210, 2015
Vintage radio speaker fabric
15 x 9 5/8 inches each

PL. 50
B-235, 2015
Vintage radio speaker fabric
11 5/8 x 4 7/8 inches each

PL. 51
B-252, 2015
Vintage radio speaker fabric
18 3/8 x 10 5/8 inches each

PL. 52
B-310, 2015
Vintage radio speaker fabric
5 1/8 x 6 7/8 inches each

PL. 53
B-288, 2015
Vintage radio speaker fabric
6 3/8 x 12 1/4 inches each

PL. 54
B-315, 2015
Vintage radio speaker fabric
11 5/8 x 8 1/4 inches each

PL. 55
B-321, 2015
Vintage radio speaker fabric
22 1/8 x 16 inches each

CONTRIBUTORS

Brett Littman is the Executive Director of The Drawing Center.

Jace Clayton is an artist and writer based in New York, also known for his work as DJ /rupture. His book *Uproot: Travels in 21st-Century Music and Digital Culture* is forthcoming from Farrar, Straus and Giroux (2016).

ACKNOWLEDGMENTS

Gabriel de la Mora: Sound Inscriptions on Fabric is made possible by the support of Sofía Anaya and Rogelio López, José Antonio García Ocejo, Cecilia Anaya and Enrique Gámez, Verónica Anaya, Sicardi Gallery, Houston, and Jack and Anne Moriniere. Additional support is provided by the Mexican Agency for International Development Cooperation (AMEXCID) with the Mexican Cultural Institute of New York and the Consulate General of Mexico in New York (SRE).

Special thanks to Timothy Taylor, London, and Proyectos Monclova, Mexico City.

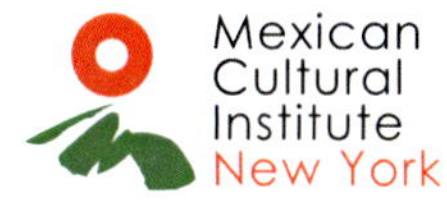

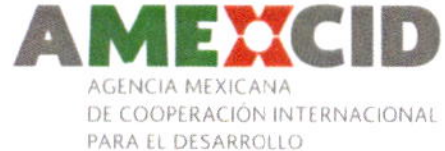

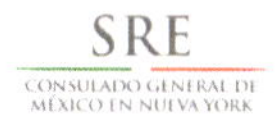

EDWARD HALLAM TUCK PUBLICATION PROGRAM

This is number 127 of the *Drawing Papers*, a series of publications documenting
The Drawing Center's exhibitions and public programs and providing a forum for
the study of drawing.

Noah Chasin *Executive Editor*
Joanna Ahlberg *Managing Editor*
Designed by AHL&CO / Peter J. Ahlberg, Kyle Chaille

This book is set in Adobe Garamond Pro and Berthold Akzidenz Grotesk.
It was printed by BookMobile in Minneapolis, MN.

ISBN 978-0-942324-97-6